LEGEND

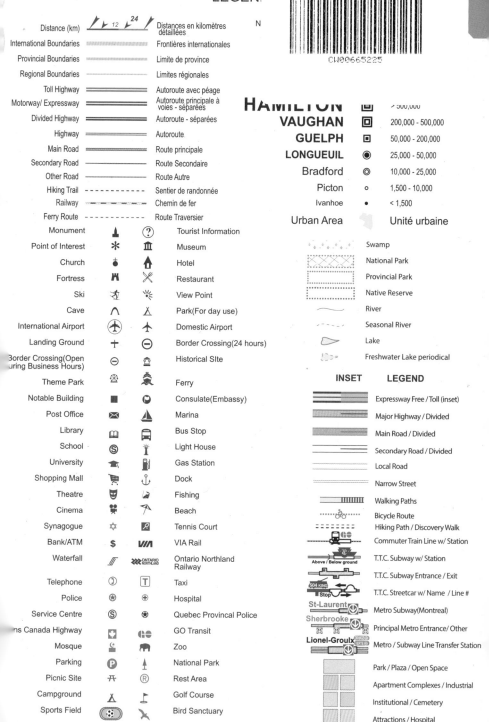

Distance (km)		Distances en kilomètres détaillées	N	
International Boundaries		Frontières internationales		
Provincial Boundaries		Limite de province		
Regional Boundaries		Limites régionales		
Toll Highway		Autoroute avec péage		
Motorway/ Expressway		Autoroute principale à voies - séparées		
Divided Highway		Autoroute - séparées		
Highway		Autoroute		
Main Road		Route principale		
Secondary Road		Route Secondaire		
Other Road		Route Autre		
Hiking Trail		Sentier de randonnée		
Railway		Chemin de fer		
Ferry Route		Route Traversier		

CW00665225

Monument	⚓	?	Tourist Information
Point of Interest	✳	🏛	Museum
Church	⛪	🏨	Hotel
Fortress	♜	🍴	Restaurant
Ski	⛷	☀	View Point
Cave	∩	⋏	Park(For day use)
International Airport	✈	✈	Domestic Airport
Landing Ground	+	⊖	Border Crossing(24 hours)
Border Crossing(Open During Business Hours)	⊖	🏛	Historical Site
Theme Park	🎡	⛴	Ferry
Notable Building	■	📍	Consulate(Embassy)
Post Office	✉	⛵	Marina
Library	📖	🚌	Bus Stop
School	Ⓢ	🗼	Light House
University	🏛	⛽	Gas Station
Shopping Mall	🛒	⚓	Dock
Theatre	🎭	🎣	Fishing
Cinema	🎬	🏖	Beach
Synagogue	✡	🎾	Tennis Court
Bank/ATM	$	VIA	VIA Rail
Waterfall	♒	ONTARIO NORTHLAND	Ontario Northland Railway
Telephone	☎	T	Taxi
Police	⊛	⊕	Hospital
Service Centre	Ⓢ	⊛	Quebec Provincal Police
Trans Canada Highway	🍁	GO	GO Transit
Mosque	☪	🐘	Zoo
Parking	P	🌲	National Park
Picnic Site	⊼	®	Rest Area
Campground	⛺	⛳	Golf Course
Sports Field	⚽	✈	Bird Sanctuary

HAMILTON	🏙	> 500,000
VAUGHAN	◙	200,000 - 500,000
GUELPH	◉	50,000 - 200,000
LONGUEUIL	●	25,000 - 50,000
Bradford	◎	10,000 - 25,000
Picton	○	1,500 - 10,000
Ivanhoe	•	< 1,500
Urban Area		Unité urbaine

	Swamp
	National Park
	Provincial Park
	Native Reserve
	River
	Seasonal River
	Lake
	Freshwater Lake periodical

INSET LEGEND

	Expressway Free / Toll (inset)
	Major Highway / Divided
	Main Road / Divided
	Secondary Road / Divided
	Local Road
	Narrow Street
	Walking Paths
	Bicycle Route
	Hiking Path / Discovery Walk
	Commuter Train Line w/ Station
Above / Below ground	T.T.C. Subway w/ Station
	T.T.C. Subway Entrance / Exit
504 KING Stop	T.T.C. Streetcar w/ Name / Line #
St-Laurent	Metro Subway(Montreal)
Sherbrooke	Principal Metro Entrance/ Other
Lionel-Groulx	Metro / Subway Line Transfer Station
	Park / Plaza / Open Space
	Apartment Complexes / Industrial
	Institutional / Cemetery
	Attractions / Hospital

ii

ONTARIO

Pages 1 - 20	Scale 1 : 1,500,000
Pages 21 - 22	Scale 1 : 750,000
Pages 22 - 62	Scale 1 : 550,000

Ontario and Quebec Elevation Bar

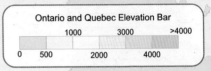

Hudson Bay

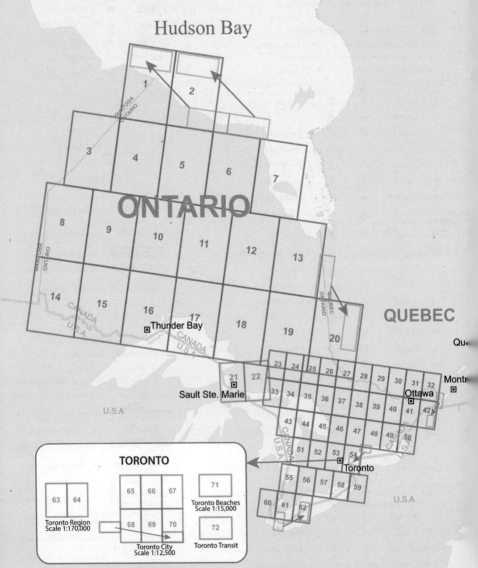

ONTARIO

QUEBEC

Thunder Bay

Sault Ste. Marie

Ottawa

Toronto

U.S.A

TORONTO

| 63 | 64 |

Toronto Region
Scale 1:170,000

| 65 | 66 | 67 |
| 68 | 69 | 70 |

Toronto City
Scale 1:12,500

| 71 |

Toronto Beaches
Scale 1:15,000

| 72 |

Toronto Transit

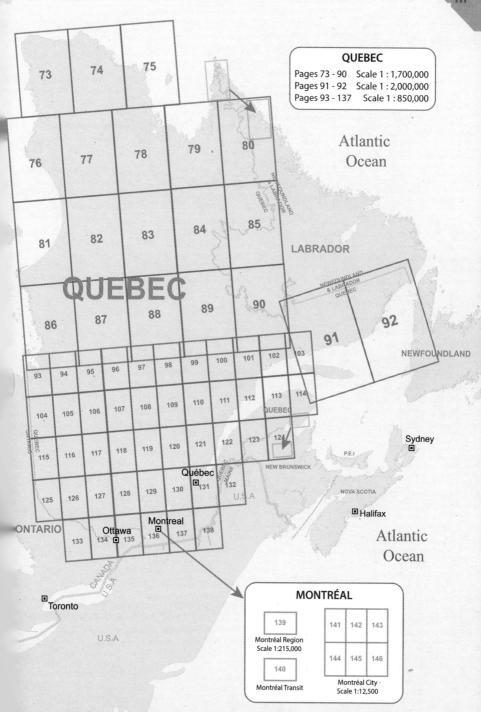

QUEBEC

Pages 73 - 90   Scale 1 : 1,700,000
Pages 91 - 92   Scale 1 : 2,000,000
Pages 93 - 137   Scale 1 : 850,000

Atlantic Ocean

73 74 75

76 77 78 79 80

81 82 83 84 85

LABRADOR

QUEBEC

86 87 88 89 90

91 92

NEWFOUNDLAND

93 94 95 96 97 98 99 100 101 102 103

104 105 106 107 108 109 110 111 112 113 114

QUEBEC

115 116 117 118 119 120 121 122 123 124

ONTARIO

Sydney

P.E.I

125 126 127 128 129 130 131 132

NEW BRUNSWICK

Québec

NOVA SCOTIA

Halifax

ONTARIO

Ottawa 134 135 136 137 138

133

Montreal

Atlantic Ocean

Toronto

CANADA
U.S.A

U.S.A

MONTRÉAL

139

Montréal Region
Scale 1:215,000

140

Montréal Transit

141	142	143
144	145	146

Montréal City
Scale 1:12,500

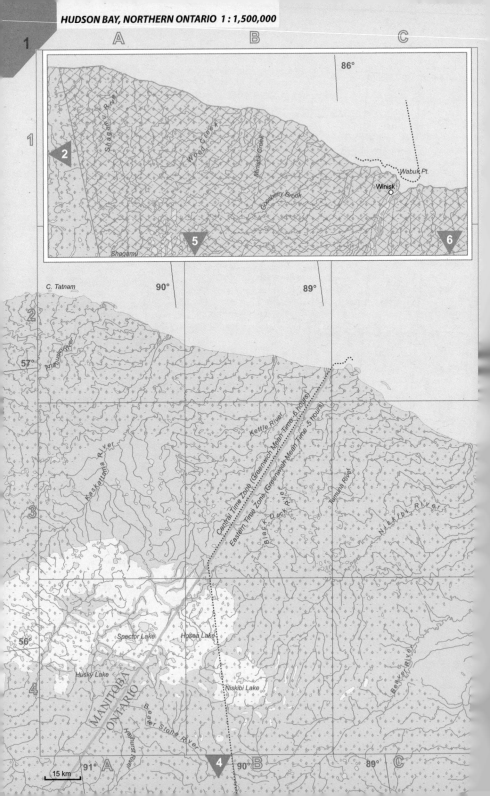

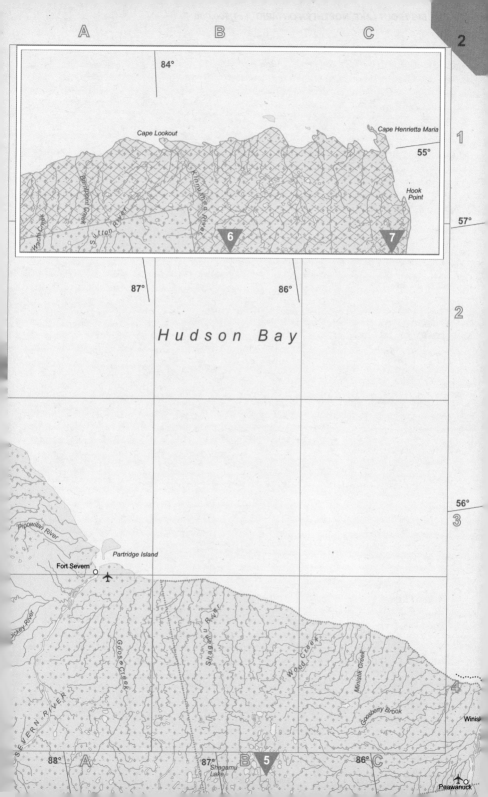

BIG TROUT LAKE, NORTHERN ONTARIO 1:1,500,000

WINISK RIVER 1 : 1,500,000

15 km

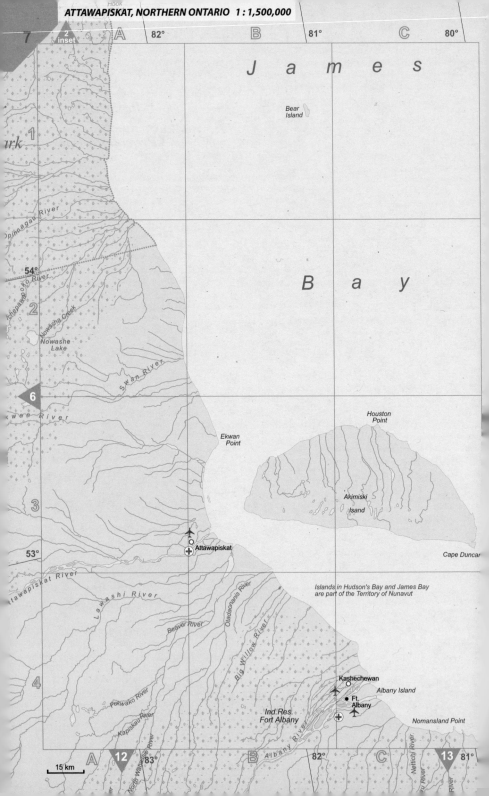

7   2 inset   A   82°   B   81°   C   80°

J   a   m   e   s

Bear
Island

rk   1

Opinnagau River

54°

Ichepanoko River

B   a   y

2

Nowasha Creek

Nowashe
Lake

Swan River

6

Ekwan
Point

kwan River

Houston
Point

Akimiski
Isand

3

53°

Attawapiskat

Cape Duncan

Attawapiskat River

Lawashi River

Beaver River

Otadaoanis River

Islands in Hudson's Bay and James Bay
are part of the Territory of Nunavut

Big Willow River

4

Pekwako River

Kapiskau River

North water River

Kashechewan

Albany Island

Ft.
Albany

Ind. Res.
Fort Albany

Nomansland Point

Albany River

Natrichi River

A   12   83°   B   82°   Albany River   C   13   81°

15 km

SANDY LAKE, NORTHERN ONTARIO 1 : 1,500,000

9   3   92°   A   91°   B   C   90°   4   Kin

Kingfisher Lake   Mana Lake

53°

Misakwash Lake   Mana Lake

Sakwaso Lake   Maggis Lake   Eyapamikama Lake   Schade Lake   Wachusk Lake

Weagamow Lake

Senia Lake   Pipestone River Prov. Park   Assin Lake

Petownikip Lake

North Caribou Lake   Akow Lake   Skinner Lake

Nikip Lake   Opakopa Lake   Weagamow Lake 367

1

323   Opapimiskan Lake   Obabigan Lake

Neawage Lake

Windigo River

McCoy Lake   Windigo Lake 366   Nango River   Donnelly Lake   Liberty Lake   Forester Lake

rry Lakes

Nango Lake

Upper Windigo Lake   Dumond P

Laughton Lake   Ochek Lake   McCauley River   Pipestone River   Pinemu   Kawin Lake   River

Pakhoan Lake

2

Kishikas Lake   Horseshoe Lake   Maneko Lake

52°

Whitestone Lake   Pipestone River Prov. Park   Obustiga Lake

Kinloch Lake   Mamiegowish Lake

8

Morris Lake   Williams Lake

Upper Gosse Lake   Bow Lake

Cat Lake   Cat Lake   Kapkichi Lake   156

Kapikik Lake   Gitche Lake   Dobie Lake   Dobie River

3

Birch Lake   Zionz Lake

rabumeni ake   Fawcett Lake   Kezik Lake   Wright Lake   Mishkeegogamang   Osnaburgh Lake

Slate Falls   New Osnaburgh   Indian Reserve

nan   Fawcett Lake   Fry Lake

Bamaji Lake   Pashkokoga Lake

ake   Perrigo Lake   Sesikinaga Lake   Blackstone Lake   Lake St. Joseph

ration   South Bay   Jeanette Lake   Greenbush Lake

Uchi Lake

51°   371   McCrea Lake

Slate Lake   Miniss Lake

Otatakan Lake   Churchill Lake

River   Whitemud Lake   De Lesseps Lake

4   599   Fitchie Lake

St Raphael Lake   Savant Lake

Adamhay Lake

Akrofoil Lake   Wapesi Lake   Kashawoegama Lake

A   92°   B   15   91°   C

15 km

357   Tully Lake   Hooker Lake

ndigo Point rovincial Park

516

Eastern Time Zone -5 hours) (Greenwich Mean Time Central Time Zone (Greenwich Mean Time -6 hours)

11   5   A   86°   B   85°   C   6

Otoskwin
Attawapiskat
Prov. Park

Kitchie
Lake
Fishtrap
Lake
Highbank
Lake

1

Streatfield River

Missisa
Lake

Kapiskau Lake

Streatfield
Lake

Kapiskau River

Lingen
Lake

Napken
Lake

Muskabik River

52°

Buffalostin River

Grander River

Muswabik
Lake

Marten Falls
(I.R.)

Ind. Res

Purcell
Lake

2

Wabassi Isle

Ogoki

Wabimeig
Lake

Albany River

Albany River
Prov. Park

Ogoki River

Ruby Creek

Albany River

10

Quartz Lake

Wash
Lake

Dusey River

Wataiaho River

atan

Little Current River

3

Dusey Lake

Little Current River

Little Drownin River

Hanley Lake

51°

Drowning River

Ragon Lake

Ogoki
Lake

Little Current River
Prov. Park

160

oki River
ov. Park

Metchett
Lake

Esnagami River

Squaw River

Ash River

Kapikotongwa Lake

Percy Lake

Legarde River

Jog Lake

Stone
Lake

Percy
Lake

Abamasagi
Lake

ra Lake

O'Sullivan
Lake

236

Marshall
Lake

Esnagami
Lake

Storm Lake

Kenogami

4

Cordingley Lake

Wababimiga
Lake

Flint River

Aroland

VIA
Nakina

Flintdale

Pagwa River

ota

Fleming
Lake

643

Lower Twin
Lake

A   87°

Upper Twin
Lake

17

B   86°   C

Murky Lake

Chipman Lake

Klotz Lake

Eureka Lake

15 km

Opaman
Lake

Burrows
Lake

68

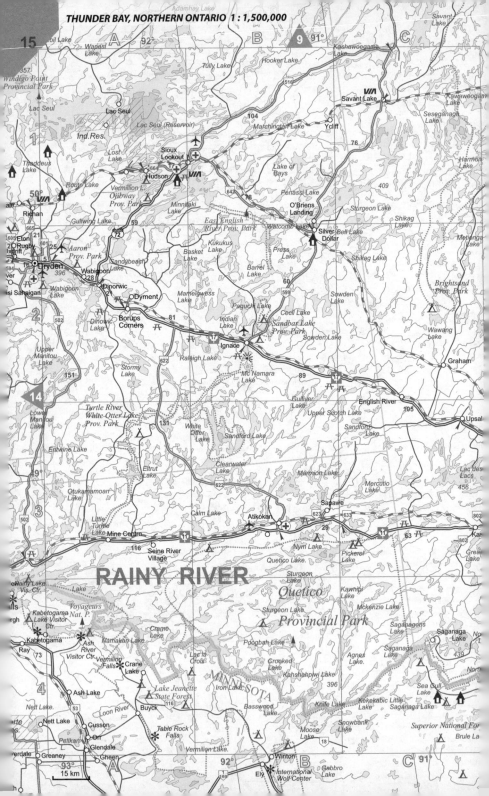

THUNDER BAY, NORTHERN ONTARIO 1 : 1,500,000

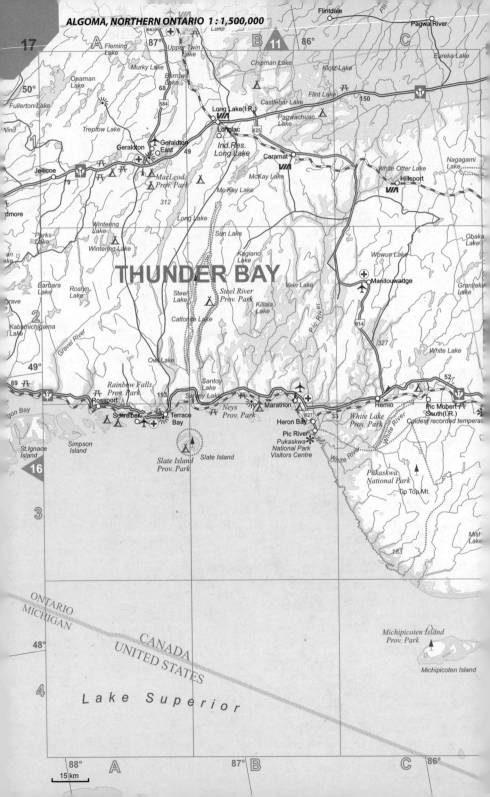

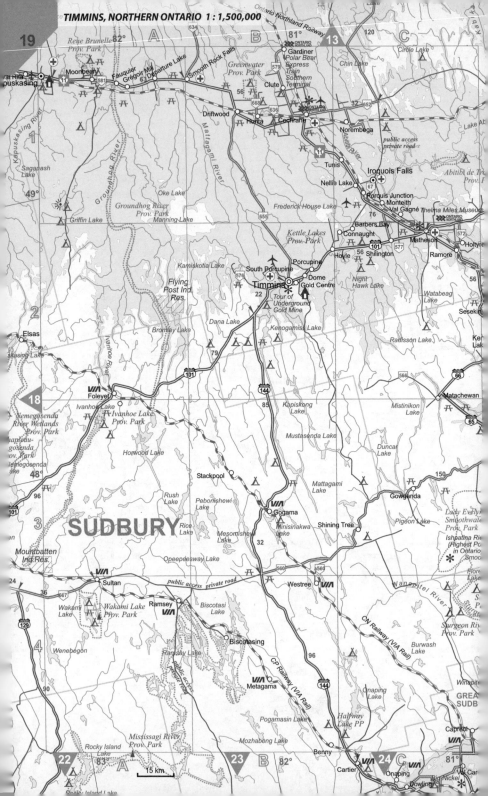

Note :
Pages 21-22 do not
have elevation data.

A

B

19

C

22

83.5°
Megisan
Lake

83°

129

Mississagi

Mississagi River Provincial Park

1

23

181

Wenebegon River

Wenebegon River Prov. Park

Aubinadong River Prov. Park

Saymo Lake

Rocky Island
Lake

47°

River

Ranger Lake

Aubrey Falls
Prov. Park

Lake au
Sables

Barr
Lake

556

Ranger Lake

Aubrey
Falls

129

River Aux Sauble
Prov. Park

2

Lake

Mississagi

River

Kirkpatrick
Lake

Rawhide
Lake

65

Wakomata
Lake

White

River

639

Mississagi
Prov. Park

Quirke
Lake

46.5°

546

Little

Industry Solid
Depot

Ophir

670

Ten Mile
Lake

3

Dunns Valley

Tunnel
Lake

Matirenda
Prov. Park

Elliot Lake

Elliot Lake

638

Wharncliffe

554

Matirenda
Lake

31

Parkinson

546

Chiblow
Lake

Mashland
Lake

42

108

Rydal Bank

Little Rapid

Day
Mills

Iron Bridge

Bruce Sta

Nestorville

33

29

Sowerby

ONTARIO
17

557

Serpent
River

Thessalon

Dayton

Dean Lake

Mississagi
River

Spragge

Cutle

aven

North Channel Islands
Prov. Park

Blind River

57

Algoma
Mills

538

Pronto East

AIRD

eph's I. MNBS

Mississagi Delta
Prov. Nature Reserve

JOHN I.

issing
y

CANADA

North Channel

4

46°

DRUMMOND
ISLAND

COCKBURN
ISLAND

Tolsmaville

BARRIE I.

A

83.5°

B

83

Sheshegwaning

C

U.S.A.

Meldrum Bay

540

540

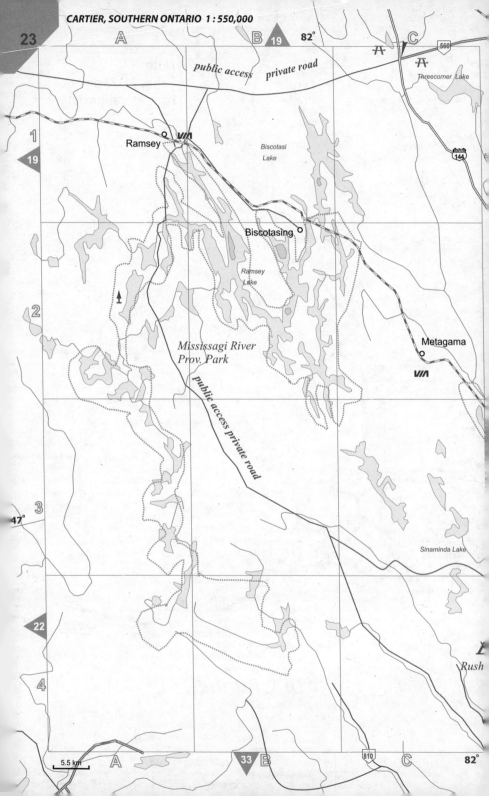

23

A

B 19 82° C

560

public access *private road*

Threecorner Lake

1
19

Ramsey

Biscotasi
Lake

Ontario
144

Biscotasing

*Ramsey
Lake*

2

*Mississagi River
Prov. Park*

Metagama

Public access private road

3

47°

Sinaminda Lake

22

4

5.5 km

A 33 B 810 C 82°

Rush

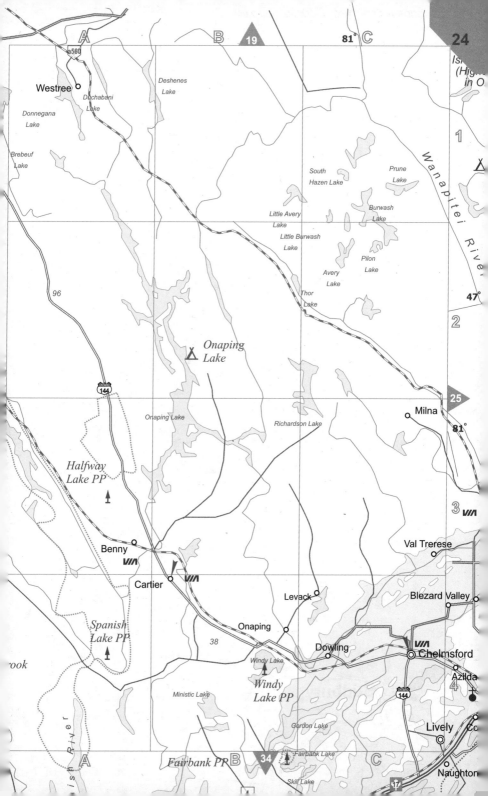

25 19 A B 20 C 80°

Barmac
Lake

* Ishpatina Ridge
(Highest Point
in Ontario)

Obabika
River
Prov. Park

Le Roche
Lake

1

Little Fry
Lake

T E M A G A

Solace
Prov. Park

Marcia
Lake

Fry
Lake

Clearwater
Lake

Upper
Bass Lake

Lake
Temagami

Obabika
Lake

47°

2

Sturgeon River PP

Emerald
Lake

Eagle
Rock
Lake

805

Laura
Lake

Chiniguchi PP

Maskinonge
Lake

81°
Milna

24

Wanapitei PP

Donald
Lake

Maskimonge
Lake

3

Wanapitei
Lake

Kukagami
Lake

Sturgeon River

VIA Capreol

Skead

Ella
Lake

Bonanza
Lake

Ashigami
Lake

al Trerese

Falconbridge

539

Blezard Valley Val Caron

Garson

535

Callum

Warren

VIA

17

72

Markstay

Hagar

125

Chelmsford

VIA

The Big Nickel

Coniston

Wahnapitae

4

Azilda

*

Ramsey
Lake

VIA

Sudbury

537

Nepewassi
Lake

St.Charles

Mashk
PP

55

Lively

Copper Cliff

Shaar
Hashomayim

Wanup

81° A

5.5 km

Naughton

Whitefish
Lake
Ind. Res.

84

Secord

35 B C

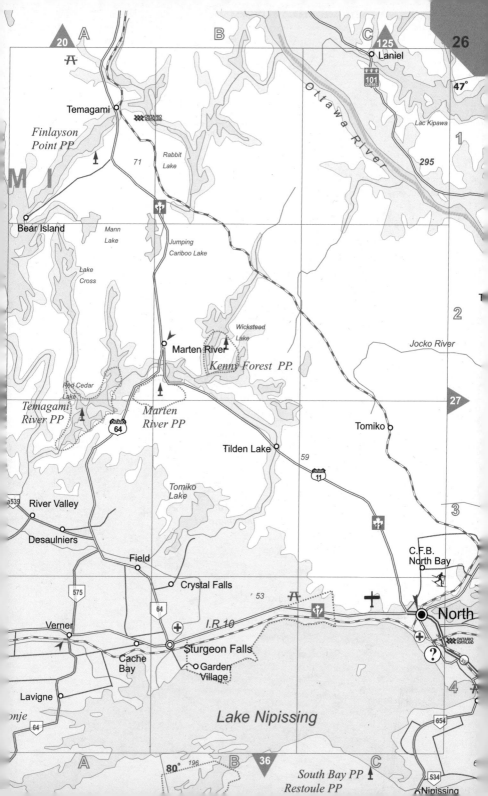

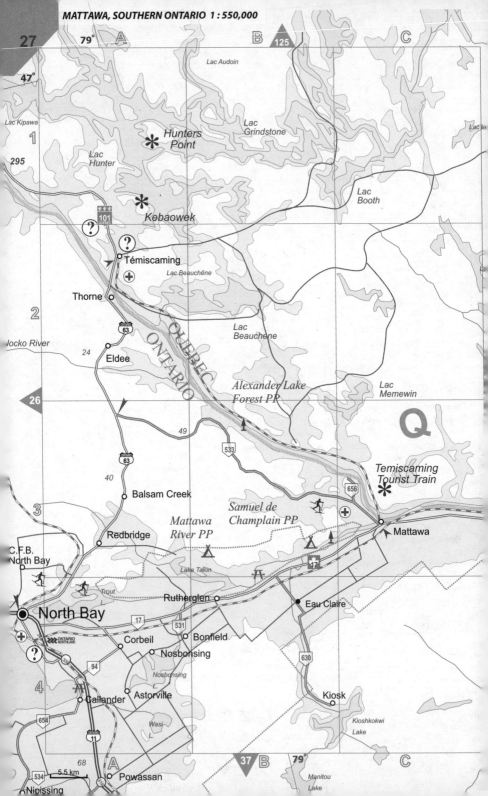

29   A 126   B 77°   C 127

Rivière Noire

1

Les Nilgaut

Lac Lynch

Rivière Coulonge

Lac Saint-Patrice

Noire R.

2

Lac Schyan

Lac de l'Achigan

Lac Galameau

L a u r

28

Lac McGillivray

Rapides-des-Joachims

635

Rolphton

Point Alexander

Deep River

3

34

Nicabong

Wa

?

Sheenboro

Chichester

Chalk River

Fort U'illiam

31

148

46°

17

Petawawa

C.F.B. Petawawa

Petawawa Point

Westmeath PP

Westm

S

Black Bay

Pembroke

26

21

28

24

4

41

Baron Canyon

Alice

62

14

56

Rankin

33

13

7

5.5 km   A   39 B   62   C

Micksburg

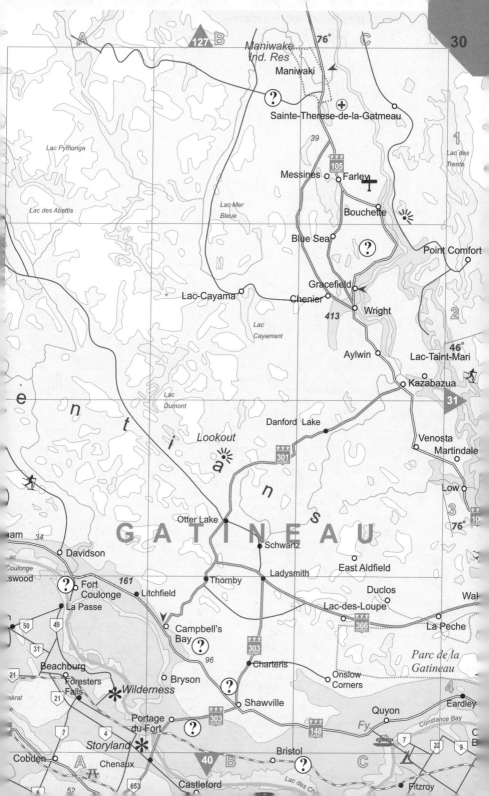

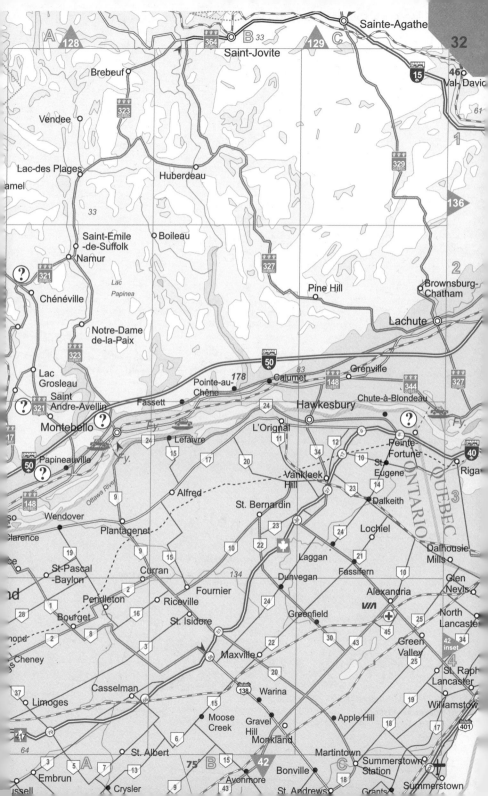

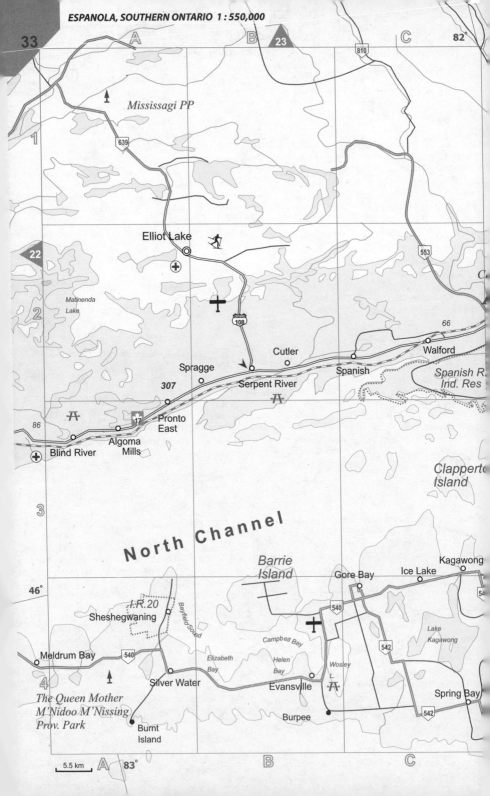

82°

A · B · 23 · C

810

Mississagi PP

639

22

Elliot Lake

553

⊕

Matinenda Lake

2

108

66

Cutler

Walford

Spragge

Spanish

307

Serpent River

Spanish R. Ind. Res

86

⊼

17

Pronto East

⊼

⊕ Blind River

Algoma Mills

Clapperton Island

3

North Channel

Barrie Island

Gore Bay

Ice Lake

Kagawong

46°

I.R. 20

Sheshegwaning

Bayfield Sound

540

54

540

Lake Kagawong

Meldrum Bay

540

Campbell Bay

542

Elizabeth Bay

Helen Bay

Wosley L.

Silver Water

Evansville

⊼

Spring Bay

4

The Queen Mother M'Nidoo M'Nissing Prov. Park

Burpee

542

Burnt Island

5.5 km   A   83°   B   C

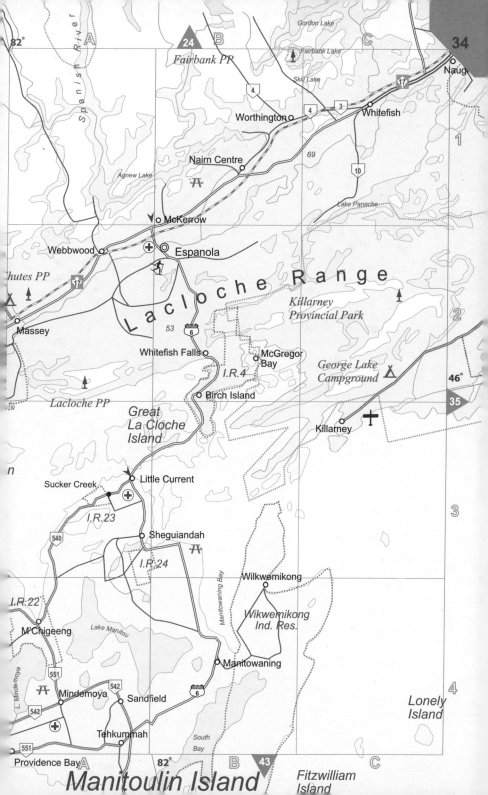

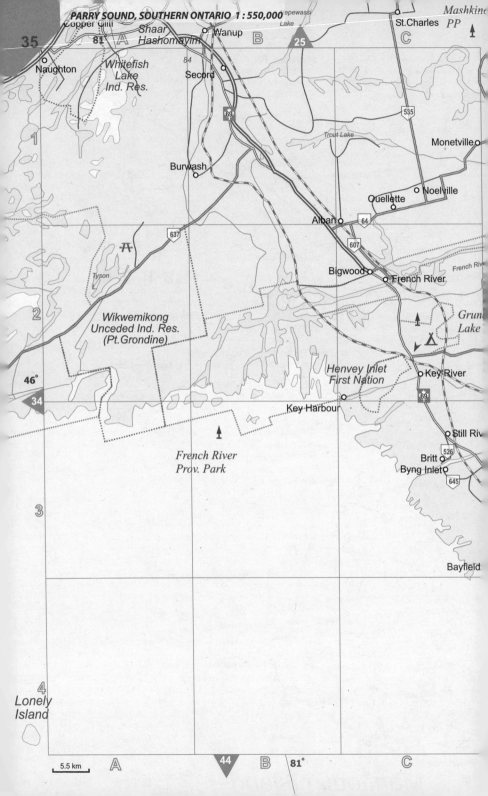

PARRY SOUND, SOUTHERN ONTARIO 1 : 550,000

Mashkine

epewassi Lake

St.Charles PP

Copper Cliff

Shaar Hashomayim

Wanup

Naughton

Whitefish Lake Ind. Res.

Secord

84

Burwash

535

Trout Lake

Monetville

Noelville

Ouellette

Alban

64

637

607

French Riv

Bigwood

French River

Tyson

Wikwemikong Unceded Ind. Res. (Pt.Grondine)

Grun Lake

46°

Henvey Inlet First Nation

Key River

Key Harbour

Still Riv

French River Prov. Park

526

Britt

Byng Inlet

645

Bayfield

Lonely Island

5.5 km

81°

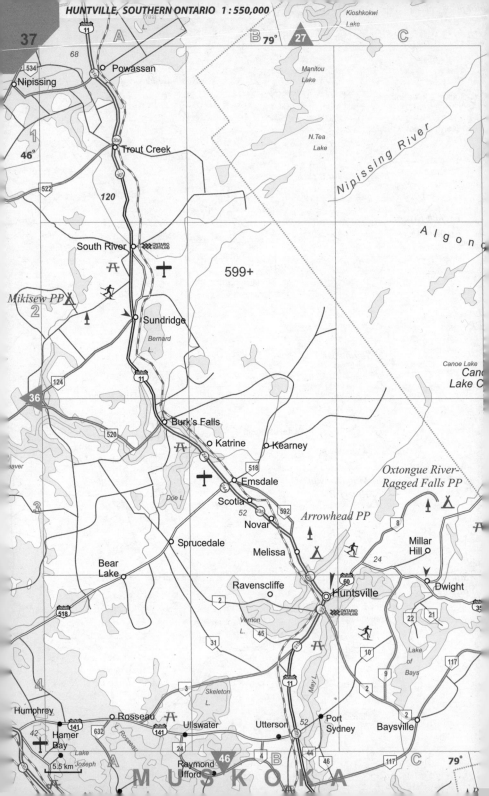

37

B 79° 27

C

68

11

Powassan

534

Nipissing

46°

306 Trout Creek

522

120

599+

Manitou Lake

N.Tea Lake

Kioshkokwi Lake

Nipissing River

Algon

South River

ONTARIO NORTHLAND

Mikisew PP

2

Sundridge

Bernard L.

124

11

36

Canoe Lake

Cano Lake C

Burk's Falls

520

Katrine

Kearney

518

Emsdale

Oxtongue River- Ragged Falls PP

Doe L.

Scotia

8

52 235 592

Novar

Arrowhead PP

aver

3

Sprucedale

Melissa

Millar Hill

Bear Lake

Ravenscliffe

2

Huntsville

Dwight

60

ONTARIO NORTHLAND

518

Vernon L.

45

24

22 21

35

31

Lake of Bays

10

9

117

3

Skeleton L.

2

Humphrey

141

632

Rosseau

May L.

11

52 Port Sydney

Baysville

2

Hamer Bay

42

Ullswater

141

Utterson

44

117

79°

24

Lake Joseph

Rosseau

Raymond Ufford

46

4

46

B

C

5.5 km

M U S K O K A

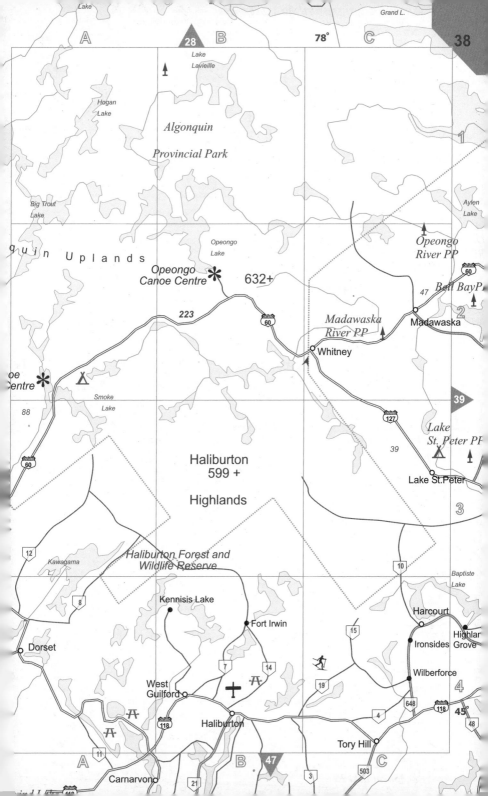

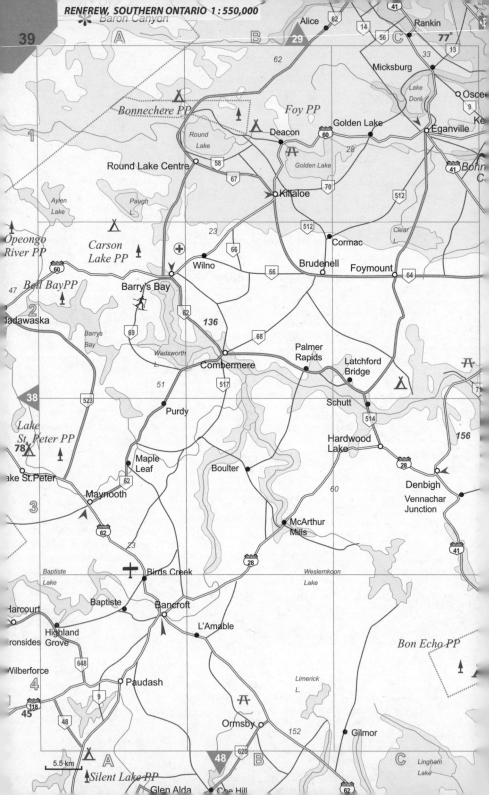

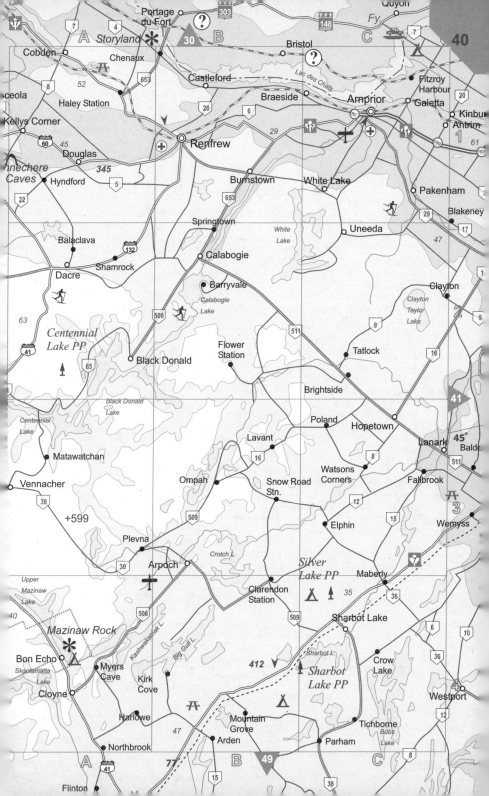

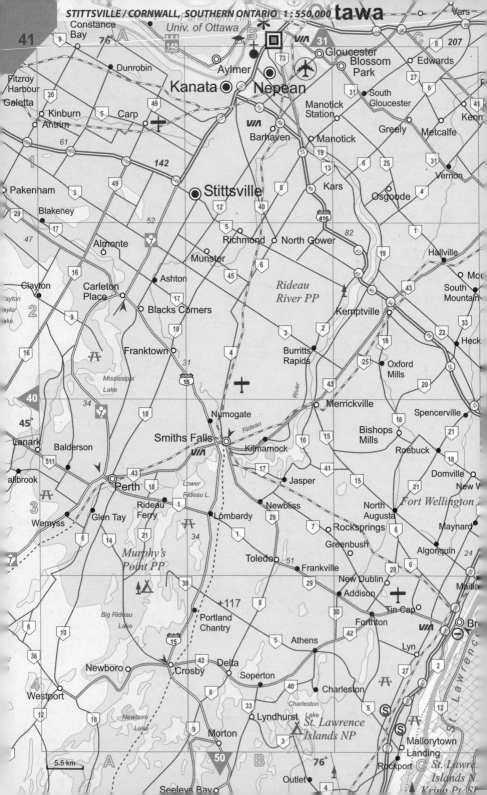

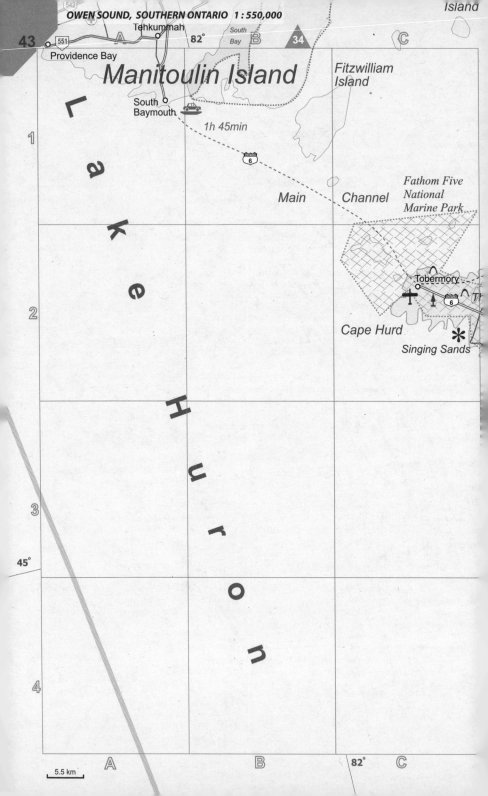

Island

43

82°

South
Bay

34

Providence Bay

Tehkummah

Manitoulin Island

South
Baymouth

1h 45min

6

Fitzwilliam
Island

1

Main   Channel

*Fathom Five
National
Marine Park*

Tobermory

6

2

Cape Hurd

Singing Sands

L a k e   H u r o n

3

45°

4

A   B   82°   C

5.5 km

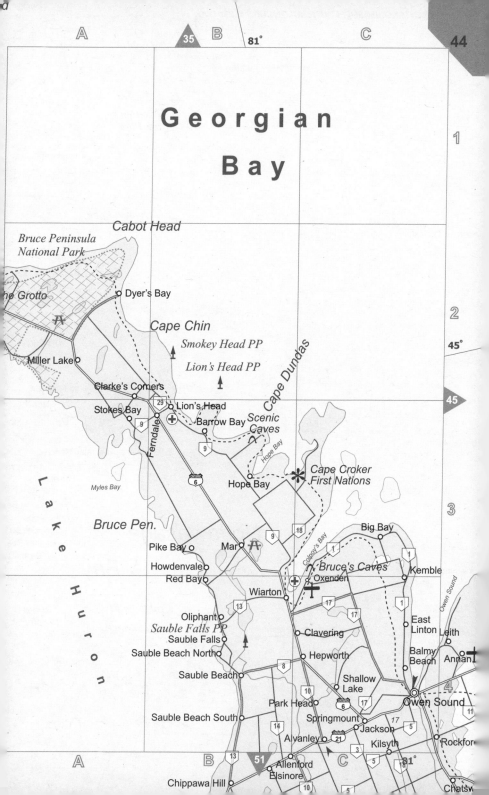

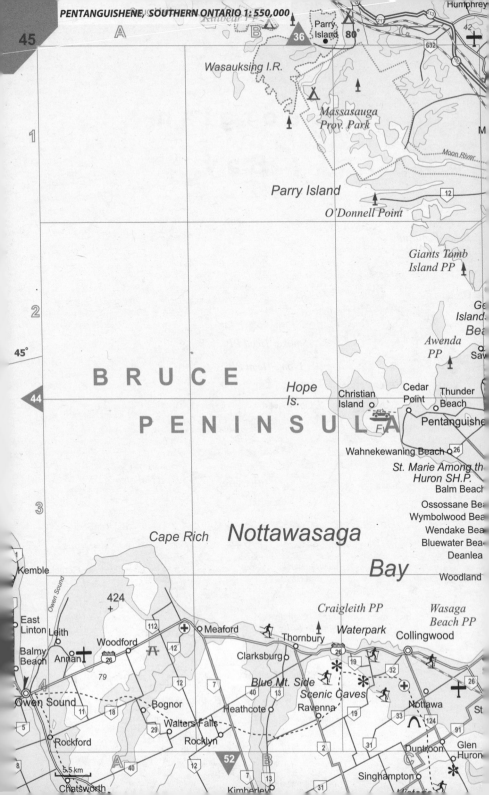

Humphrey

Parry Island **80°**

Wasauksing I.R.

36

Massasauga Prov. Park

Parry Island

O'Donnell Point

12

Giants Tomb Island PP

Island

1

Moon River

Ge Island Bea

Awenda PP

Sav

2

Hope Is.

Christian Island

Cedar Point

Thunder Beach

B R U C E

P E N I N S U L A

Pentanguishe

44

45°

Wahnekewaning Beach **26**

St. Marie Among th Huron SH.P.

Balm Beach

Ossossane Be

Wymbolwood Bea

3

Cape Rich

Nottawasaga

Wendake Bea

Bluewater Bea

Deanlea

Bay

Woodland

Craigleith PP

Wasaga Beach PP

1

Kemble

424

Meaford

Thornbury

Waterpark

Collingwood

112

Woodford

12

Clarksburg

26

East Linton

Leith

Annan

26

79

12

7

Blue Mt. Side Scenic Caves

40

13

19

32

26

4

Balmy Beach

Owen Sound

Bognor

Heathcote

Ravenna

19

Nottawa

11

18

124

91

5

Rockford

Walters Falls

29

Rocklyn

2

31

33

Duntroon

Glen Huron

8

5.5 km

A

40

52

12

B

7

Singhampton

Chatsworth

Kimberley

13

31

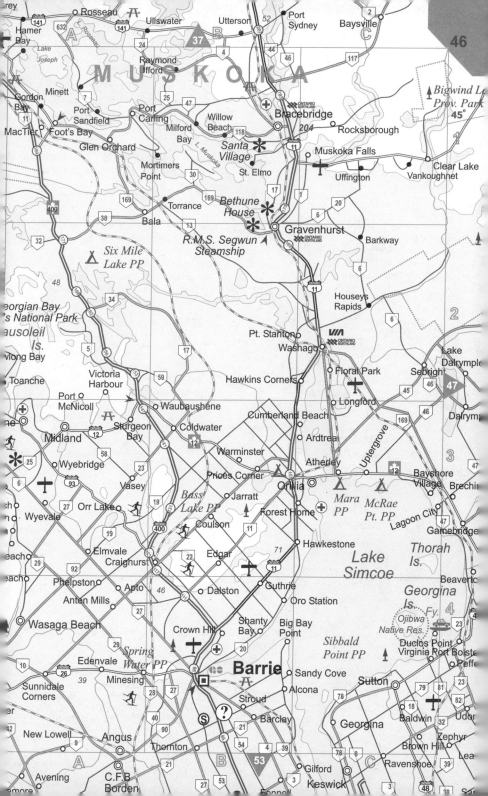

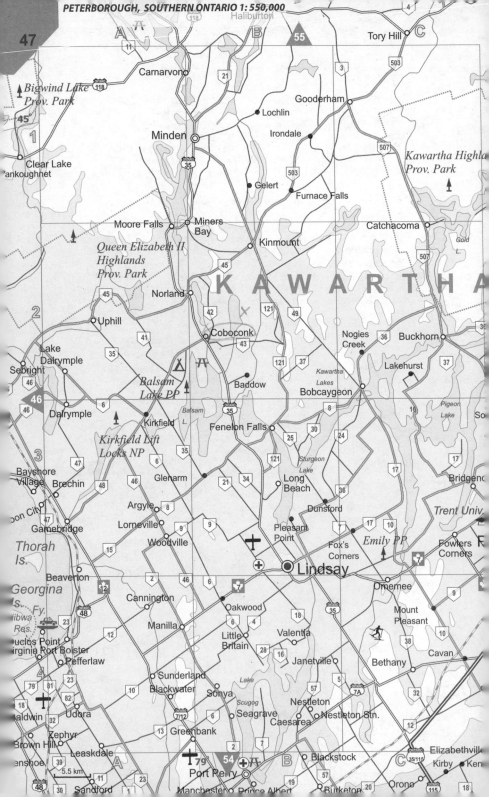

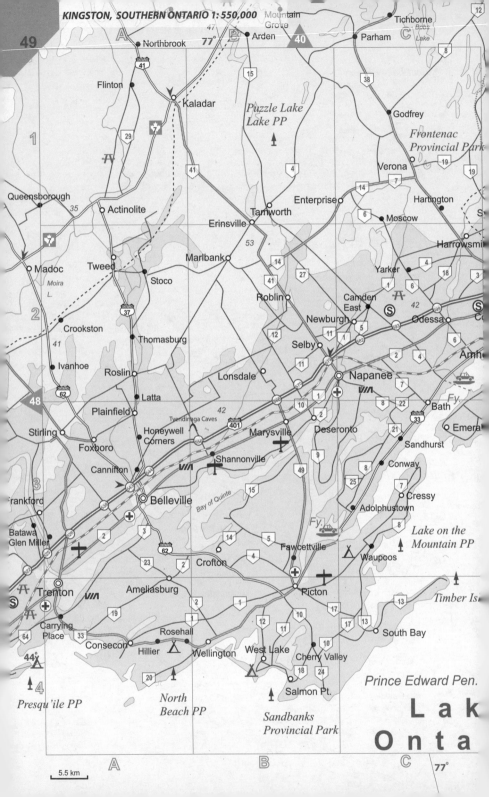

49

40

12

Tichborne

Bobs Lake

Mountain Grove

Arden

Parham

Northbrook

8

77°

47

41

Flinton

15

38

Kaladar

Godfrey

29

7

Puzzle Lake
Lake PP

Verona

19

Frontenac
Provincial Park

4

19

Queensborough

35

Actinolite

41

Tamworth

Erinsville

14

Enterprise

7

Hartington

6

Moscow

Harrowsmi

Madoc

Moira L.

Tweed

Stoco

Marlbank

53

14

41

27

Roblin

Yarker

1

6

18

3

37

Crookston

Thomasburg

12

Camden
East

Newburgh

S

42

Odessa

S

Co

Ivanhoe

Roslin

11

Selby

5

11

1

6

48

62

Latta

Plainfield

42

Tyendinaga Caves

11

Lonsdale

10

Napanee

2

4

Amh

7

Fy

Bath

Stirling

Honeywell
Corners

Foxboro

401

Marysville

1

8

22

21

33

Emera

Cannifton

VIA

Shannonville

2

9

Deseronto

Sandhurst

Conway

7

Cressy

Belleville

Bay of Quinte

15

49

8

25

8

Adolphustown

8

Lake on the
Mountain PP

rankford

14

5

Fawcettville

Waupoos

Batawa
Glen Miller

2

3

62

Crofton

4

Picton

17

Timber Is

13

Trenton

VIA

Ameliasburg

2

1

10

17

13

South Bay

23

2

19

Rosehall

12

11

17

64

Carrying
Place

33

Consecon

Hillier

Wellington

West Lake

10

Cherry Valley

10

24

44°

Salmon Pt.

18

Prince Edward Pen.

20

North
Beach PP

Sandbanks
Provincial Park

L a k

O n t a

Presqu'ile PP

4

77°

A

B

C

5.5 km

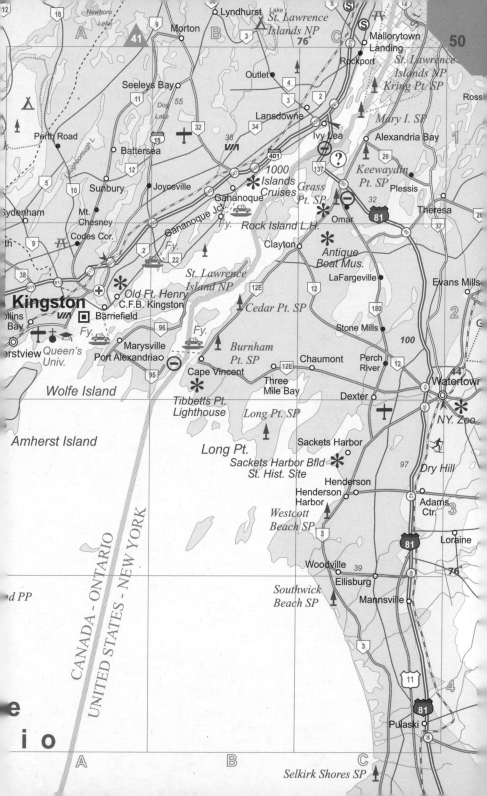

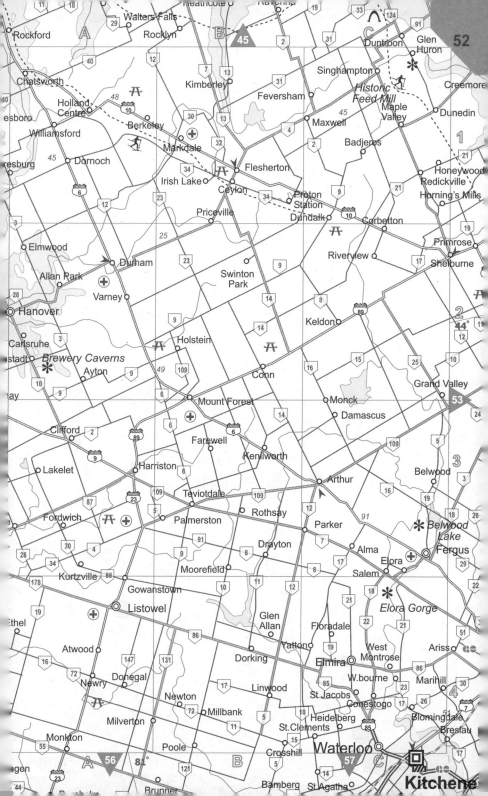

A

B

51

C

Octagonal
Downtown

20

31

15

8

18

Holmesville

Vana

13

L
a
k
e

H
u
r
o
n

Bayfield

3

129

1

St. Joseph

84

Z

ONTARIO
21

83

Grand Bend

Pineridge Zoo

81

2

Port Sanilac
*Sanilac
Co. Mus.*

*Pinery
Provincial Park*

5

Cor

Port
Franks

Ipperwash Beach

Northville

18

Kettle Point

Thedford

7

25

Kettle Pt. Concretions

6

Port Sanilac

Arkona

Richmondville

12

Forest

12

Ke

3

33

Forester

7

79

9

Lexington

ONTARIO
21

Warwick

22

Lexington
Heights

30

11

ONTARIO
402

44

Kerwo

Camlachie

102

34

39

Lakeport

7

Brights
Grove

Watford

Lakeport SP

Point
Edward

15

25

Reeces Corners

39

9

37

Wyoming

43°

1

6

21

79

Port Huron

VIA

Mandaumin

39

VIA

8

27

Sarnia

14

Lucasville

26

4

Lucasville

20

Petrolia

Alvinston

69

Marysville

Oil City

Inwood

80

Corunna

31

*Oil Museum
of Canada*

Mooretown

ONTARIO
40

80

61

Oil Springs

82°

Ca

A

B

C

5.5 km

Courtright

Edys Mills

Oakdale

Shetland

79

St. Clair

36

UNITED STATES - MICHIGAN
CANADA - ONTARIO

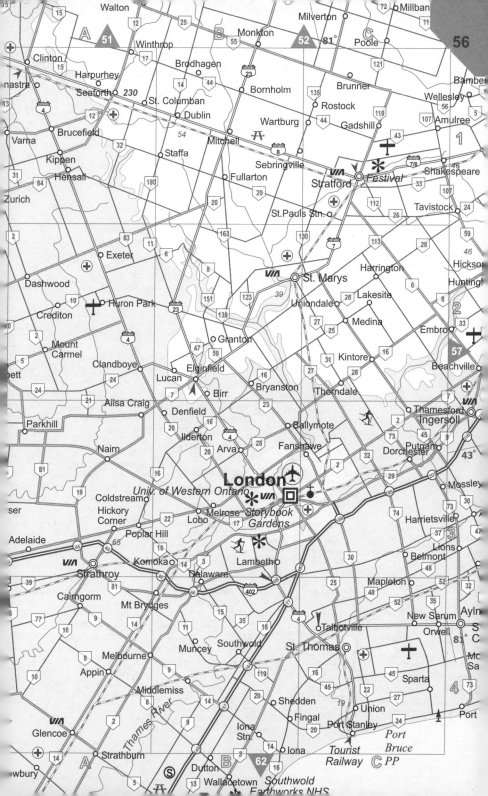

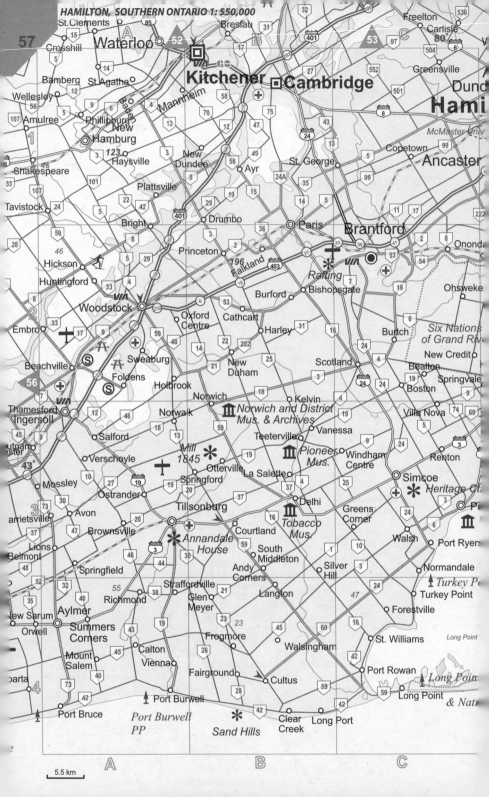

Waterdown
1
154
B
53
Historic Pioneer Settlement
54
C
58
Burlington
VIA
Aldershot
Dundas
Hamilton
403
Fruitland
Stoney Creek
Grimsby
VIA
St. Catharines
QEW
55
Jordan
VIA
?
Homer
51
Thorold
89
Vinemount
Vinyard Area
Winona
47
78
74
64
81
Vineland
Campden
St.
Jordan
Thorold South
1
Elfrida
450
411
Beamsville
Mount
Hope
6
633
Woodburn
20
Fulton
Grassie
12
14
St. Anns
18
69
24
Fenwick
Fonthill
406
Tonawanda
In
Welland
43°
56
Smithville
Bismarck
Binbrook
622
65
65
20
29
Caluke
33
Caistor
Centre
14
27
Wellandport
63
Dain City
58A
84
Empire
Corners
Caistorville
2
Chambers
Corners
23
58
140
Caledonia
9
Canborough
221
Wainfleet
Gasline
York
56
Canfield
15
3
Ostryhon
Corners
Port Colborne
Willow
Grove
29
6
54
Grand River
9
65
66
Lowbanks
Long
Beach
3
Burnaby
Middleport
48
Cayuga
32
Dunnville
Byng
Hagersville
52
17
11
Port Maitland
Nelles Corners
20
Kohler
20
50
49
South
Cayuga
Rock
Point PP
59
Townsend
Fisherville
8
Rainham
Centre
Jarvis
53
Cheapside
18
55
3
70
62
Nanticoke
Selkirk PP
Port Dover
Harbour
Mus.
E r i
3
Point PP
E
Lake
Erie SP
4
Long Point
90
20
National Wildlife Area
Westfield
A
80°
B
C
May

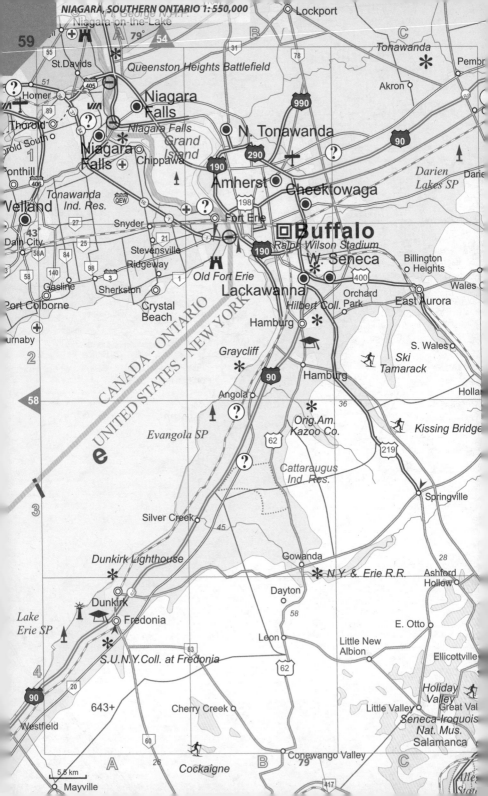

55

Oil Museum
of Canada

Oil City
Inwood
Oil Springs

Mooretown

Courtright

St. Clair
Marine City
Sombra

New Haven

Anchorville

Algonac S.P.

Algonac
Walpole

MACOMB

Selfridge ANG Base

Edys Mills
Oakdale
Shetland
Cairo

Wilkesport

Rutherford

Florence

Port Lambton

Croton

Tupperville
Dresden
Wabash
Thames

Wallaceburg

Site of Uncle
Tom's Cabin

Kent
Bridge

McKay's
corners

Bkejwanong Territory
Walpole Is. First Nation

Eberts

Louisville

Dover Centre

Pinehurst

Mitchell's Bay

Chatham

Grande Point

401

Lake
St. Claire

Pain Court

Blenhe

Prairie
Siding

Charing
Cross

Stoney Point
Lighthouse Cove

Jeannettes
Creek

Links of
Kent GC.

Erie

Tecumseh
St. Clair Beach
Puce
Emeryville
Belle River
Deerbrook

North
Buxton

Fletcher

Dealtown

Tilbury

Merlin

St. Joachim

195

Comber

Port Alma

Elmstead

Ruscom
Station

North
Woodslee

Watkins
Glen SP.

Essex
South
Woodslee

Staples

Maidstone

Cottam

Blytheswood

Wheatley

Wheatley PP

Gesto

77

Holiday Harbour

Minor Bird
Sanctuary

Ruthven

Leamington

Kingsville

Seacliffe

Point Pelee
National Park

Harrow

Oxley

Linden Beach
Cedarhurst Park
Cedar Beach

Colchester

5.5 km

To Scudder and
Pelee Island

62
inset

Pt. Pelee

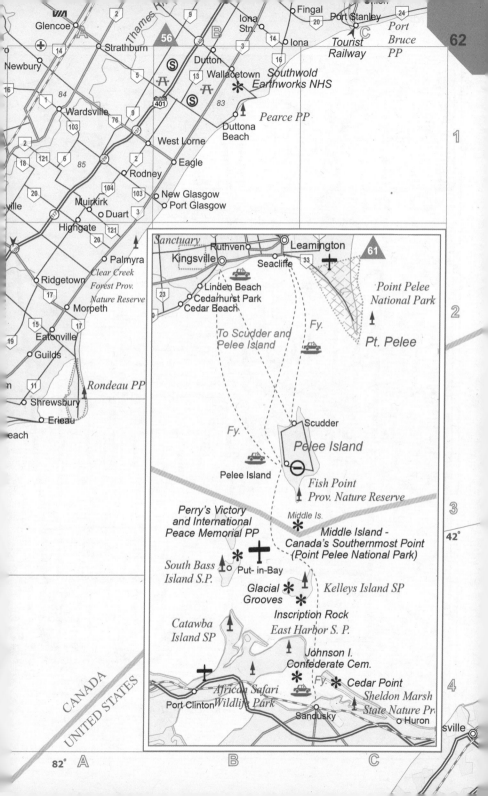

VIA

Glencoe A

Strathburn

Newbury

Wardsville

84

76

West Lorne

Eagle

Rodney

New Glasgow
Port Glasgow

Muirkirk
Duart

Highgate

Palmyra

Ridgetown

Morpeth

Eatonville

Guilds

Shrewsbury
Erieau

each

Clear Creek Forest Prov. Nature Reserve

Rondeau PP

Thames R.

56

401

S

S

Dutton

Wallacetown

13

Iona
Stn.

14

Iona

16

Fingal

20

Port Stanley C

Tourist
Railway

Port
Bruce
PP

62

*Southwold
Earthworks NHS*

Duttona
Beach

Pearce PP

83

1

2

Sanctuary

Kingsville

Ruthven

Seacliffe

Leamington

33

61

*Point Pelee
National Park*

Linden Beach
Cedarhurst Park
Cedar Beach

23

Fy.

*To Scudder and
Pelee Island*

Pt. Pelee

2

Fy.

Scudder

Pelee Island

Pelee Island

⊘

*Fish Point
Prov. Nature Reserve*

3

42°

*Perry's Victory
and International
Peace Memorial PP*

Middle Is.

*Middle Island -
Canada's Southernmost Point
(Point Pelee National Park)*

*South Bass
Island S.P.*

Put- in-Bay

*Glacial
Grooves*

Kelleys Island SP

*Catawba
Island SP*

Inscription Rock
East Harbor S. P.

Johnson I.
Confederate Cem.

Fy.

Cedar Point

*Sheldon Marsh
State Nature Pr*

*African Safari
Wildlife Park*

Port Clinton

Sandusky

Huron

sville

4

CANADA

UNITED STATES

82° A

B

C

Barrie, Sudbury, North Bay

MAPLE

McMichael Canadian Art Collection

Canada's Wonderland

Maple

RUTHERFORD RD.

Natl. Golf Club

Aloft Vaughan Mills

Vaughan Mills Mall

Reptilia

RUTHERFORD RD.

RI

VAUGHAN

LANGSTAFF RD.

LANGSTAFF RD.

LANGSTAFF RD.

HIGHWAY 7

Country Golf Club

400

Don Valley

Thornhill Regional Park

CENTRE ST.

Thornhill Country Golf Cl.

11

Vaughan City Centre

HIGHWAY 7

HIGHWAY 7

THORNHILL

WOODBRIDGE

407

407 TOLL HIGHWAY

CN

427

27

Hwy. 401/Oakville

407

STEELES AVE.

STEELES AVE.

Black Creek Pioneer Village

York Stadium

STEELES AVE.

STEELES AVE.

Wild Water Kingdom

Humber Valley Park

FENMAR DR.

Sanofi Pasteur

Ross Lord Park

CN

York

York University

Gibson House

North York Ctr. Perf. Arts

NORTH Y CENTRE

Fin

ALBION RD.

FINCH AVE. W.

FINCH AVE. W.

FINCH AVE. W.

FIN

BRAMPTON

REXDALE

Humber River

BATHURST ST.

Downsview

DOWNSVIEW

SHEPPARD AVE.

SHEPPARD AVE.

NORTH YORK

4C

MARTIN GROVE RD.

KIPLING AVE.

ISLINGTON AVE.

ALBION RD.

WESTON RD.

JANE ST.

DOWNSVIEW

Earl Bales Park

Malton

Woodbine Racetrack

Humber Valley Golf Club

Oakdale Golf Club

Downsview Park

ALLEN DR.

Ski Hill

York

HIGHWAY 27

GO

400

WILSON AVE.

Downsview Airport

WILSON AVE.

HOG NOLL

Airport Hotels

Etobicoke N.

401

Yorkdale Shopping

AVENUE RD.

Yonge Subway

CARLINGVIEW DR.

409

DIXON RD.

Weston

LAWRENCE AVE. W.

University/Spadina Subway

LAWRENCE PAR

11A

11

Pearson Toronto Int'l Airport

427

27

THE WESTWAY

JANE ST.

BLACK CREEK DR.

KEELE ST.

DUFFERIN ST.

ALLEN EXWY.

BATHURST ST.

Sunny

ETOBICOKE

EGLINTON AVE. W.

EGLINTON AVE. W.

EGLINTON AVE. W.

Kid Re Hosp.

Guelph, London

401

Scarlett Woods Golf Club

YORK

Yonge / Eglinton

Davisville

EGLINTON AVE. W.

ERINDALE

RATHBURN RD.

Smythe Park

WESTON RD.

FOREST HILL

Mt. Pleasant Cemetery

MT. PLEASANT

Upper Canada

Contenial Park Golf Club

Islington Golf Club

ST. CLAIR AVE. W.

St. Clair LRT

Spadina Mus.

CP

BURNHAMTHORPE RD.

DUNDAS ST. W.

THE JUNCTION

DUPONT ST.

427

ISLINGTON

Montgomery's Inn

Humber Valley Park

5

HIGH PARK

Bloor Subway

AVENUE RD.

ROSEDALE

SIX POINTS

BLOOR ST. W.

TRANSIT

Bloor

Cloverdale Mall

DUNDAS ST. W.

JANE ST.

KEELE ST.

DUFFERIN ST.

Royal Ontario Museum

BLOOR ST. W.

BLOOR ST.W.

5

CP

High Park

TORONTO

YONGE ST.

III

BLOOR ST. E.

Kipling

SWANSEA

PARKSIDE DR.

RONCESVALLES

GO CP

DUNDAS ST. W.

SPADINA AVE.

UNIVERSITY

JARVIS ST.

Sherway Gardens

THE QUEENSWAY

GARDINER EXWY.

PARKDALE

QUEEN ST. W.

First Canadian Place

KING ST. W.

KING ST. E.

Dixie

QUEENSWAY

Mimico

Humber Bay

CN

GO CP

Exhibition

Old Fort York

FRONT ST.

Union

GARD

Evans Ave.

QEW

Maintenance Ctr.

Humber Bay Park

Western Beaches

LAKESHORE BLVD.

QUEENS QUAY

Toront Harbo

Toronto Golf Club

LONG BRANCH

MIMICO

LAKESHORE BLVD.

Ontario Place

Toronto Island Airport

MISSISSAUGA

Long Branch

Marie Curtis Park

Colonel Sam Smith Park

Long Branch Park

LAKE ONTARIO

Toronto Island Park

TORONTO ISLANDS

Toronto City Map Coverage See Pages 65-70

2

1.6km

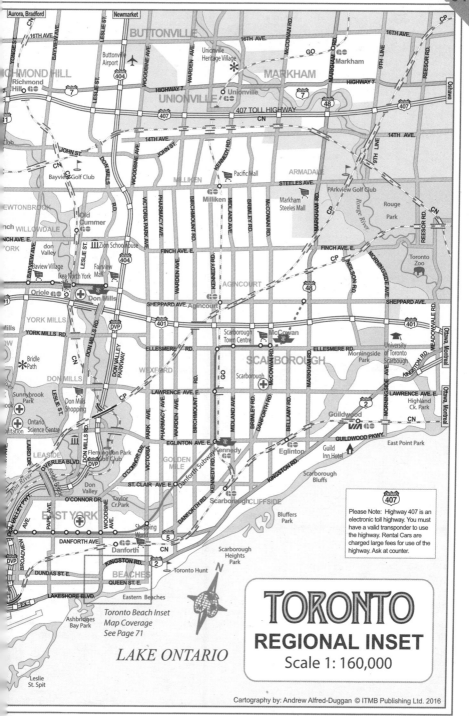

TORONTO
REGIONAL INSET
Scale 1: 160,000

Please Note: Highway 407 is an electronic toll highway. You must have a valid transponder to use the highway. Rental Cars are charged large fees for use of the highway. Ask at counter.

Toronto Beach Inset Map Coverage See Page 71

LAKE ONTARIO

Cartography by: Andrew Alfred-Duggan © ITMB Publishing Ltd. 2016

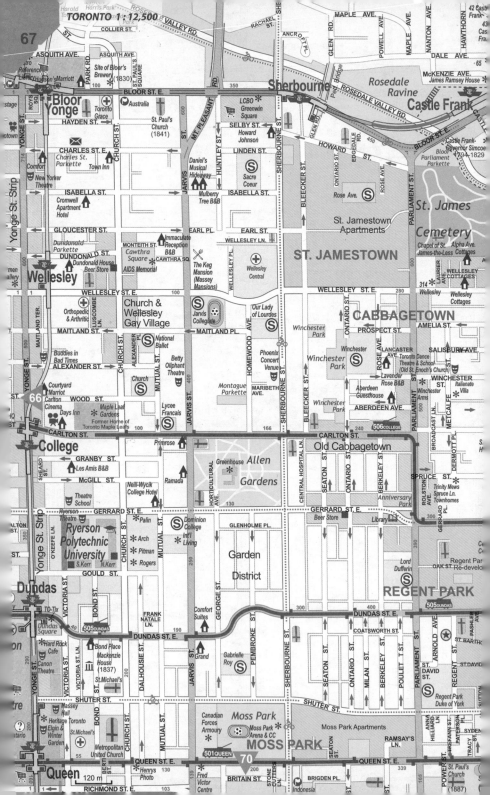

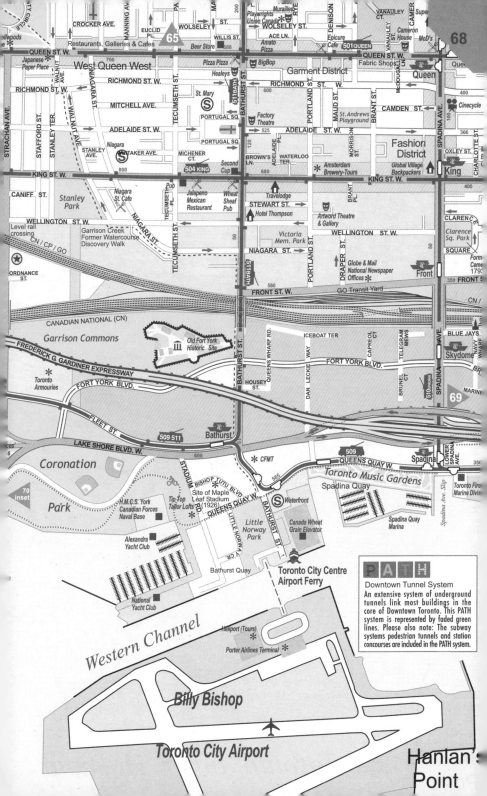

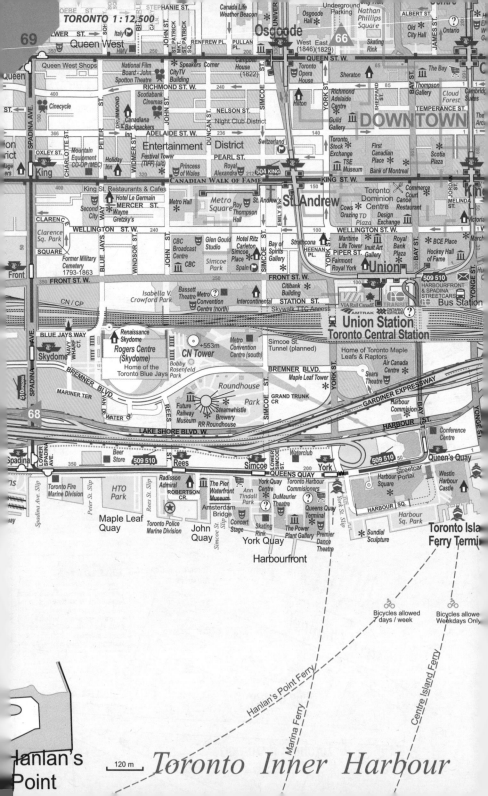

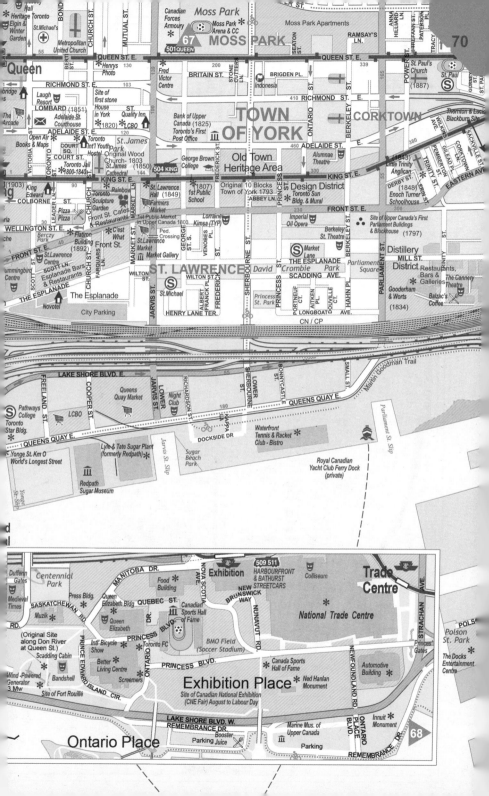

71

TORONTO
Beaches Inset
Scale 1 : 15,000
©ITMB Publishing Ltd. 2016

THE BEACHES

LAKE ONTARIO

BLANTYRE AVE.
VICTORIA PARK AVE.
VICTORIA PARK AVE.
BINGHAM AVE.
NEVILLE PARK BLVD.
KINGSWOOD RD.
SCARBOROUGH RD.
SILVER BIRCH AVE.
WILLOW AVE.
BEECH AVE.
SPRUCE HILL RD.
BALSAM AVE.
SYCAMORE PL.
WINTHORPE RD.
SOUTHWOOD DR.
WINEVA AVE.
HAMBLY AVE.
LEE AVE.
WHEELER AVE.
BELLEFAIR AVE.
WAVERLEY RD.
KENILWORTH AVE.
ELMER AVE.
HERBERT AVE.
WOODBINE AVE.
RAINSFORD RD.
BROOKMOUNT RD.
LOCKWOOD RD.
NORTHERN DANCER BLVD.
EDGEWOOD AVE.
HIGHCROFT RD.

KINGSTON RD.
QUEEN ST. E.

Glen Stewart Park
Kew Beach Park
Beaches Park
Balmy Beach
Kew Gardens
Woodbine Park
Woodbine Beach
Ashbridge's Bay Park

NEVILLE PARK BLVD.
NURSEWOOD RD.
MUNRO PARK AVE.
GLENFERN AVE.
FERNWOOD AVE.
MACLEAN AVE.
GLEN MANOR
SCARBORO BEACH BLVD.
HAMMERSMITH AVE.
WINEVA AVE.
LEUTY AVE.
LEE AVE.
WAVERLEY RD.
KENILWORTH AVE.
KIPPENDAVIE AVE.
BULLER AVE.
BOARDWALK DR.
JOSEPH DUGGAN RD.
SARAH ASHBRIDGE AVE.
WINNERS CIR.
LAKESHORE BLVD. EAST

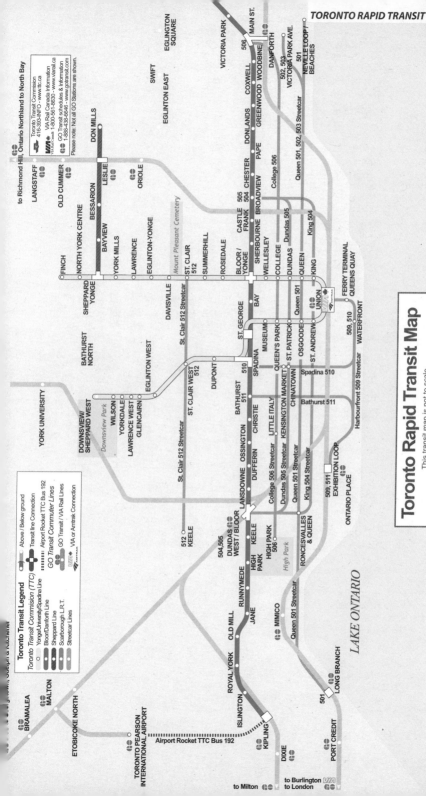

Toronto Rapid Transit Map

This transit map is not to scale.

Cartography by: Andrew Duggan   © ITMB Publishing Ltd. 2016

73

A 78°   77° **B**   HUDSON STRAIT   76°   **C**

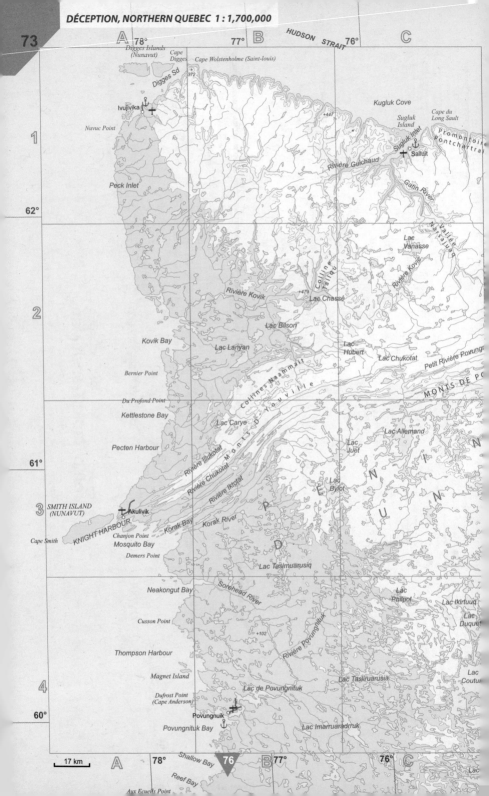

Digges Islands (Nunavut)
Cape Digges
Cape Wolstenholme (Saint-louis)
•372

Ivujivika
Kugluk Cove
•447
Suglук Island
Cape du Long Sault
Sugluk Inlet
Salluit
Promontoir Pontchartrai

Nuvuc Point

1

Rivière Guichaud
Gatin River

Peck Inlet

62°

Lac Vanasse
Collines Tallau
Navsaluaq
Vallée

Rivière Kovik
•479
Lac Chassé
Rivière Kovik

Lac Bilson

2

Kovik Bay
Lac Lanyan
Lac Hubert
Lac Chukotat
Petit Rivière Povung
MONTS DE PC

Bernier Point

Du Profond Point
Collines Naammit
Monts D Youville

Kettlestone Bay
Lac Carye
Lac Allemand

Pecten Harbour
Rivière Illukotat
Lac Juet

61°
Rivière Chukotat
Rivière Iкtotal
Lac Bylot
P   E   N   I   N

3 SMITH ISLAND (NUNAVUT)
Akulivik
Korak Bay
Korak River
U   N

KNIGHT HARBOUR
Chanjon Point
Mosquito Bay
P

Cape Smith
Demers Point
D

Lac Tasimuarusiq

Neakongut Bay
Sorehead River
Lac Philpot
Lac Ikirtuuq

Cusson Point
Lac Duquet
•102
Rivière Povungnituk

Thompson Harbour

Magnet Island
Lac Tasliruarusia
Lac Coutur

4

Dufrost Point (Cape Anderson)
Lac de Povungnituk

60°
Povungnuik

Povungnituk Bay
Lac Imarruaradruk

Lac

| 17 km | **A** | 78° | Shallow Bay | **▽ 76** | **B** 77° | | 76° | **C** |

Reef Bay

Aux Ecueils Point

Charles Bay

Cape de
Nouvelle-France
74°
Cape Moses Oates

B   73°

72° C

Charles Island
(Nunavut)

Pointe Radisson
Weggs Island

Davies Island

1

Déception
Bay

Vallée
Arquialuk

Foul Bay

Prémontoire
de Martigny

Pinnacle Islands

62°

Lac
Duquet

Déception

Rivière Déception

Maiden Island

Ivanhoe Island

Douglas
Harbour

Wales Island

Lac
Françoys-
Malherbe

Purtuniq

Lac
Watts

+561

Mont Obs
The Helmet

Cape La Potherie

Fisher Bay

Cape
Akuliagattaq

Wakeham Bay

+561

Mt. Albert Law

Doctor Island

Kattiniq

Kangiqsujuaq

2

Lacs Nuvilic

Rivière Wakeham

Joy Bay

Pointe Frontenac
Tuttle Point
Burgoyne Bay

Lacs Esker

Whitley Bay

VUNGNITUK

Rivière Povungnituk

Bégon Point
De Coulong
Point

Cratère du Nouveau- Québec
*

E

75

61°

Lac
Rouxel

+657

S
U
U
V
A

+566

Lac Nantais

3

Lac
Pennault

Lac Desdiguières

Lac
Headwind   Lac Calme

Lac Kloiz

Lac
Aggautik

Lac Châtelain

Rivière Lepelle

Rivière Vachon

Rivière Bu

Lac
Fairwind

Rivière Lesdage

Lac Bécard

Rivière Arnaud (Payne)

60°

4

Lac du
Pelican

Lac
Qalluviartuuq

A   **77**

74°

B   73°

C   72°   **78**

Lac
Brünel

Lac
Jérémie

Lac
Wesp

Lac
Tasiaalujjuaq

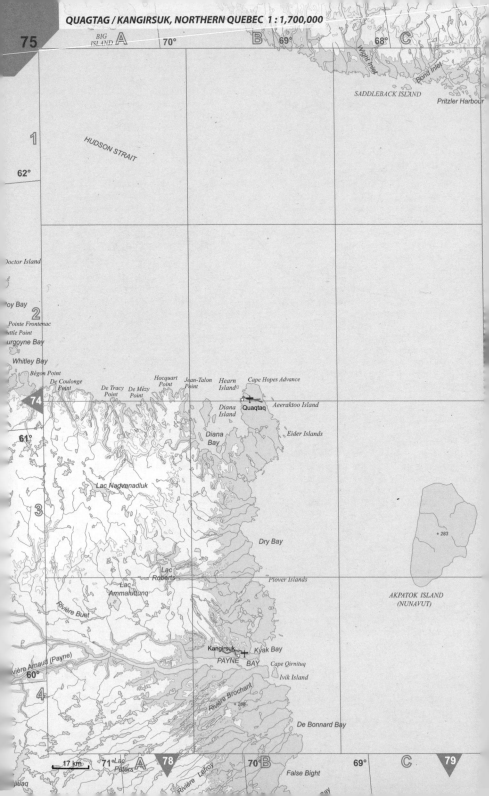

75

BIG ISLAND A   70°   B   69°   68° C

Wyatt Inlet

Bond Inlet

SADDLEBACK ISLAND

Pritzler Harbour

1

HUDSON STRAIT

62°

Doctor Island

oy Bay

2

Pointe Frontenac

ittle Point

urgoyne Bay

Whitley Bay

Bégon Point

De Coulonge Point

De Tracy Point

De Mézy Point

Hocquart Point

Jean-Talon Point

Hearn Island

Cape Hopes Advance

74

Diana Island

Quaqtaq

Aeeraktoo Island

61°

Diana Bay

Eider Islands

Lac Nagvanadluk

3

Dry Bay

+ 283

Lac Roberts

Lac Ammaluttung

Plover Islands

AKPATOK ISLAND (NUNAVUT)

Rivière Buet

Kangirsuk   Kyak Bay

PAYNE   BAY   Cape Qirnituq

Rivière Arnaud (Payne)

60°

Ivik Island

4

Rivière Brochant

+ 26

De Bonnard Bay

17 km   71° Lac Peters A   78   B   70°   69°   C   79

Rivière Lefroy

False Bight

Povungnituk

Povungnituk Bay

Lac Inukuluk

| A | 79° | | 78° | B | 73 | 77° | C | | 76 |

Shallow Bay

Reef Bay

Aux Ecueils Point

Boucher Point

Lac Kogaluc

+40

SHOAL HARBOUR

Lac Neakunguak

Lac Mangnuc

Rivière Kogaluc

1

Bourjoli Point

Kogaluk Bay

Mistake Bay

59°

Despins Point

Rivière Manet

Commodore Island

PENINSULE D'UNGAVA

Rivière Naiberakhyiik

Rivière Koktac

2

Elsie Island

Portland Promontory

Cox Island

Cape Dufferin

McCormack Island

Rivière Innuksuac

Young Island

WITCH BAY

Rivière Kongut

Inukjuak (Port Harrison)

Lac Scoter

+164

77

Patterson Island

HOPEWELL SOUND

Lac Nuluachlovik

Harrison Island

Fraley Island

Frazier Island

HOPEWELL

Drayton Island

Leonard Island

ISLANDS

Normand Point

Bartlett Island

Rivière Kikkerteluc

3

Bell Harbour

58°

copeet ds

HUDSON BAY

Cotter Island

Lac Bush

BAIE D'HUDSON

Rivière Boniface

McTavish Island

Rivière Longland

Beach Island

Husky Island

Broughton Island

+472

UT)

DRIFTWOOD ISLAND

NASTAPOCA

Nicholson Island

4

ISLANDS

Davieau Island

Nastapoka Sound

The Throat

KING GEORGE ISLANDS

Lac Tikkerutu

Point of Baleine Blanche

| land | 79° | A | | 78° | B | 81 | 77° | C | | |

Mowat Island

Christie Island

Rivière M

AUPALUK, NORTHERN QUEBEC 1 : 1,700,000

77

73

A

60°

B

74°

74

C

73°

Lac du Pelican

Lac Parry

Lac Qalluviartuuq

Lac Brunel

Lac Jérémie

Lac Button

Lac Wesp

Rivière Arnaud (Payne)

1

Rivière Kogaluc

Lac Payne

Lac Anuc

Lac Tasiat

Lac Pavy

Lac Tassialouc

59°

Rivière Manet

Lac Serin

Lac Vernon

Lac Pullison

Lac Kelsey

Lac Bellot

Lac Sabi

2

Lac le Roy

Lac Bisson

Lac Dune

Lac Yourin

Lac La Chevrolière

Lac Bartie

Lac Rochelor

Le Marc

76

ac Nuluachlovik

Vallée Narsaaluk

Lac Chavigny

Lac Bacqueville

Lac Maguire

+465

58°

Rivière Innuksuac

3

Lac Bush

Rivière aux Feuilles

Rivière Longland

Lac Quilinuarpaluk

L Ne

Deception Bay

4

Lac Minto

Lac Tikkerutuc

Rivière Longland

— 17 km

A

60°

82

B

74°

C

73°

Lac de Serr

Rivière Nastapoka

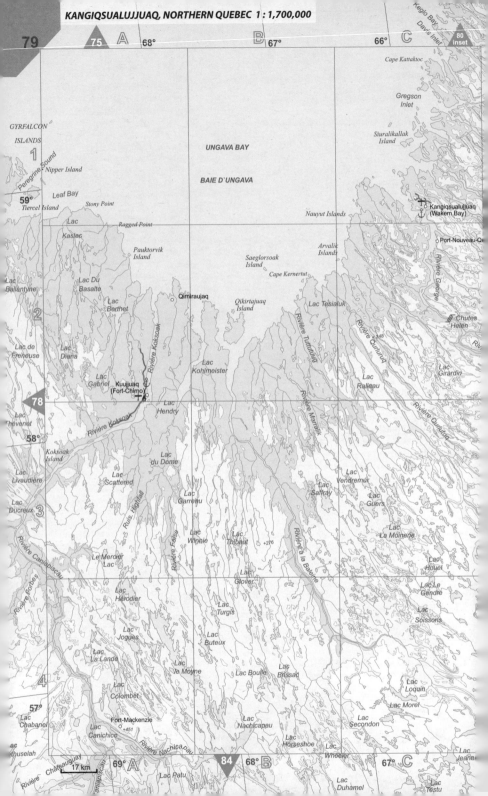

KANGIQSUALUJJUAQ, NORTHERN QUEBEC 1 : 1,700,000

79   75   A   68°   B   67°   66°   C   80 inset

Keglo Bay
Davis Inlet

Cape Kattaktoc

Gregson Inlet

Siuralikallak Island

GYRFALCON ISLANDS

1

Peregrine Sound

Nipper Island

UNGAVA BAY

BAIE D'UNGAVA

Kangiqsualujjuaq (Wakem Bay)

59°
Tiercel Island
Leaf Bay
Stony Point

Port-Nouveau-Qt

Lac Kaslac

Ragged Point

Nauyut Islands

Rivière George

Lac Ballantyne

Pauktorvik Island

Saeglorsoak Island

Arvalik Islands

Lac Du Basalte

Qimiraujaq

Qikirtajuaq Island

Cape Kernertut

Lac Tasialuk

Chutes Helen

2

Lac Berthet

Lac Diana

Rivière Koksoak

Lac Kohimeister

Rivière Tunulitug

Rivière Qurlutuq

348

Lac Girardin

Lac de Freneuse

Lac Gabriel
Kuujjuaq (Fort-Chimo)

Lac Ralleau

78

Lac Hendry

Rivière Marralik

Rivière Qurlutuq

Lac Thévenet

Rivière Koksoak

58°

Koksoak Island

Lac du Dome

Lac Livaudière

Lac Scattered

Ruis. Highfall

Lac Vendremur

Lac Saffray

Lac Guers

Lac Ducreux

3

Lac Garreau

Rivière Caniapiscau

Rivière Felse

Lac Winnie

Lac Thibaut
+276

Rivière à la Baleine

Lac La Moinerie

Le Mercier Lac

Lac Houel

Rivière Forbes

Lac Glover

Lac Le Gendre

Lac Herodier

Lac Turgis

Lac Soissons

Lac Joques

Lac Buteux

4

Lac La Lande

Lac Je Moyne

Lac Boulle

Lac Brissac

Lac Loquin

Lac Morel

Lac Colombet

57°

Lac Chabanel

Fort-Mackenzie
+451

Lac Nachicapau

Lac Secondon

ac Musthuselah

Lac Canichico

Rivière Nachicapau

Lac Horseshoe

Lac Wheeler

Lac Jeanne

Rivière Châteauguay

17 km

69° A

84

68° B

67° C

Lac Patu

Lac Duhamel

Lac Testu

80
Inset

Alluviaq
Fiord

65° A 64° B Nachvak Bay 63° C 62°

Komaktorvik
Lake

Fiord

Atlantic Time

Eastern Time

Chasm
Lake

Nachvak

Nachvak Fiord

Crest of
Watershed

Koroc River

1621+

Riviere Koroc

+1093 Chute
Korluktok

Ruis Sukaliuk

+974

+1207

+777

Québec

Lac
Tasirlaq

LABRADOR
QUÉBEC

Riviere Ford

e George

Les
Pyramides

+591

Lac
Henrietta

Colline
Wedge

Collines
Hadès

Riviere George

Ruis Slippery

Ninawawe

+529 Lac
Coiffier

Lac
Guérard

A 65° B

Lac
de la
Hutte

Lac Napu-Kainlus

85

64°

Gray Strait

Killiniq

Killiniq Island Knight Islands Lacy Island

Cape William Smith NUNAVUT

Port Burwell QUÉBEC Cape Chidley Islands

Goddard Island McLelan Strait

Shunqmiyuk Home Island

Tunnissugjuak

Ikkudliayuk
Fiord Ikkudliayuk
Fiord Avayalik
Islands

60°

Noodleoo
Fiord Ekortiarsuk
Fiord

Inlet Odell
Lake

Bell Inlet

Bray Inlet Lac
Sheppard Eclipse River

MOUNTAINS

Le Droit Point +370

58°

QUÉBEC

Weymouth Inlet

Kegio Bay Fiord
Alluviaq

Davis Inlet

Alluviaq
Fiord

79 65° 80

Siorak Brook

Martin
Island Oka

Saputit Lake

North River

Umiakovik
Lake Lake
Tasiuyak Tasialua

+1033 Frank Lal

Sikkoyavik Brook Laura Lal

57°

Kingurutik River

Tasialuk Lake

Fraser River Tasiuak Lake

Anaktalik Brook

Cabot Lake

Sipukat
Lake

1

2

3

4

C 63°

Kogaluk River

 this River

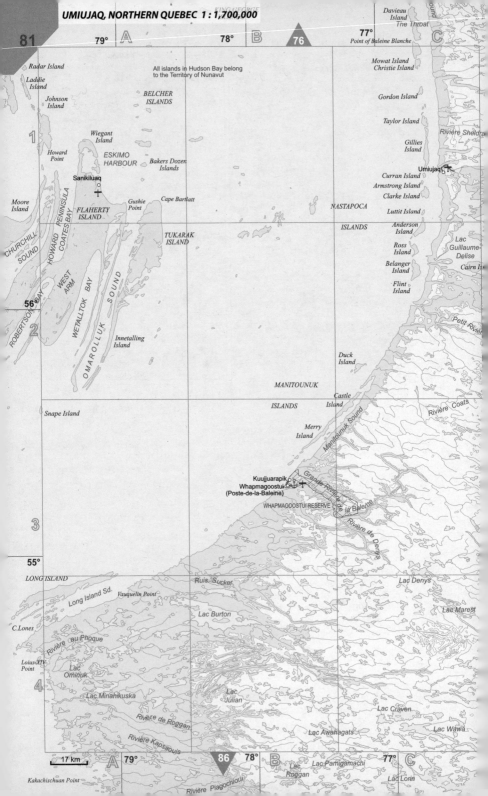

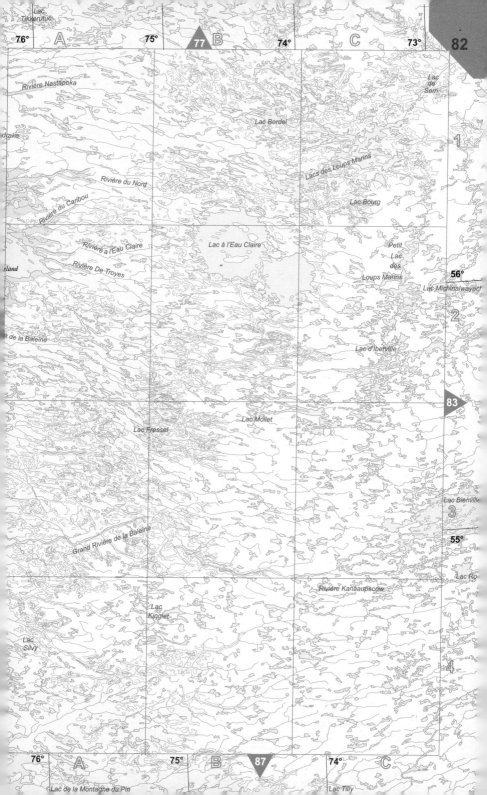

83

A   72°   B   71°   78   C   70°

Rivière aux Mélèzes

Lac Chabanel

Lac Desbergères

Lac Methuselah

Lac de Sem

Rivière Delay

Rivière du Gué

Rivière Châ

1

Lac Vallerenne

Lac Châteauguay

Lac De Noue

Lac Loudin

Lac Moyer

Lac Kaminapiskwasi

56°

Lac Michinalwayach

Lac Mondélac

2

Lac Gayot

Lac Favard

82

Lac Mannessier

Lac Vaujours

Sé

Lac Lartigue

Lac Chastenay

Lac Rome

Lac Biresallas

Lac Bienville

Lac Cognac

4

3

Lac Ossant

Lac Neret

55°

Lac De La Noue

Lac Roc

Lac Chastelain

Lac Fontanges

Lac Robutel

Brisay

Lac Chauils

Fontanges

Lac Vauleza

Lac Herve

Lac Brisay

Lac Vincilotte

4

Lac Vinet

Lac Maingard

Lac Hurault

Réservoir de La Grand 4

Lac Niaux

Lac Maic Ottor

Laforge

Lac Holmer

Lac de Lohiver

Lac Desnambuc

17 km

A   72°   88   B   71°   C

Lac Des Voeux

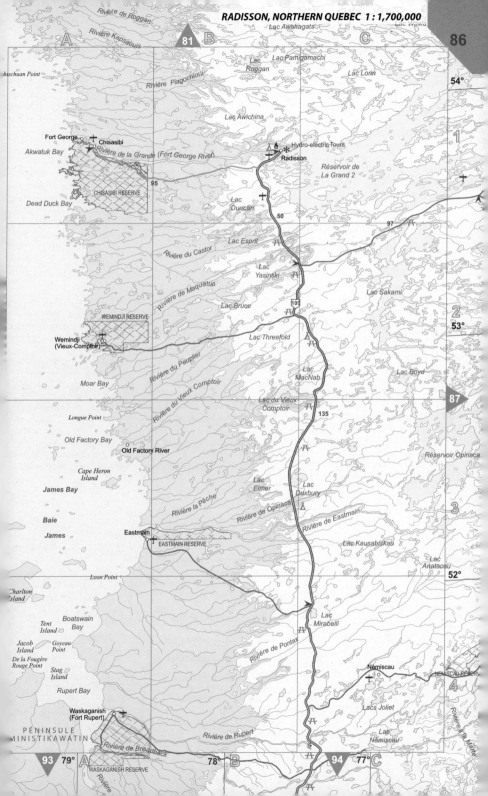

Lac Awahagats
Lac Wawa
Lac Craven

A
B
C

Rivière de Roggan
Rivière Kapsaouis
Lac Pamigamachi
Lac Roggan
Lac Lorin

hischuan Point
Rivière Piagochioul

54°

Lac Awichina

1

Fort George
Chisasibi
Hydro-electric Tours

Akwatuk Bay
Rivière de la Grande (Fort George River)
Radisson

95
Réservoir de
La Grand 2

CHISASIBI RESERVE

Dead Duck Bay
Lac Duncan

50

Rivière du Castor
Lac Esprit

97

Lac Yasinski

Rivière de Maquatua
109

Lac Bruce
Lac Sakami

WEMINDJI RESERVE

2
53°

Wemindji
(Vieux-Comptoir)
Lac Threefold
Lac Boyd

Moar Bay
Rivière du Peuplier
Lac MacNab

Rivière du Vieux Comptoir
Lac du Vieux
Comptoir

Longue Point
135

Old Factory Bay
Réservoir Opinaca

Old Factory River

Cape Heron
Island
Lac
Elmer
Lac
Duxbury

James Bay
Rivière la Pêche

Baie
Rivière de Opinaca

James
Rivière de Eastmain

3

Eastmain
Lac Kausabiskau

EASTMAIN RESERVE
Lac
Anatacau

Loon Point
52°

Charlton
sland

Boatswain
Bay
Lac
Mirabelli

Tent
Island

Jacob
Island
Goyeau
Point

De la Fougère
Rouge Point
Rivière de Pontax

Stag
Island
Némiscau
NEMISCAU RESERVE

Rupert Bay
4

Waskaganish
(Fort Rupert)
Lacs Joliet

PÉNINSULE
Lac
Némiscau

MINISTIKAWATIN

79°
A
WASKAGANISH RESERVE
Rivière de Broadback
78°
B
77°
C

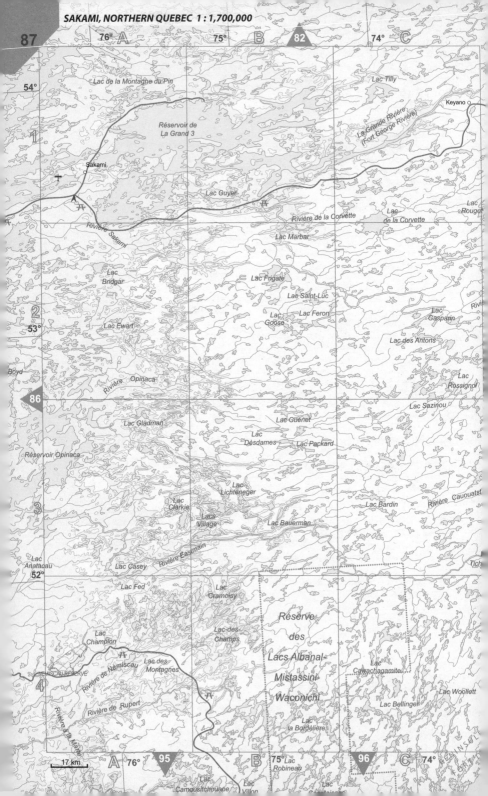

54°

76° A   75° B   82   74° C

Lac de la Montagne du Pin

Lac Tilly

Keyano

1

Réservoir de
La Grand 3

La Grande Rivière
(Fort George Rivière)

Sakami

Lac Guyer

Lac
Rouge

Lac
de la Corvette

Rivière de la Corvette

Rivière Sakami

Lac Marbar

Lac
Bridgar

Lac Frigate

Lac Saint-Luc

Lac
Gaspann

2

53°

Lac Ewart

Lac
Goose

Lac Feron

Lac des Antons

Boyd

Rivière Opinaca

Lac
Rossignol

86

Lac Sazinou

Lac Gladman

Lac Guénet

Réserve Opinaca

Lac
Désdames

Lac Packard

Lac
Lichteneger

Lac Bardin

Rivière Cauouatst

3

Lac
Clarkie

Lacs
Village

Lac Bauerman

Lac
Anatacau

52°

Lac Casey

Rivière Easimain

Tich

Lac Fed

Lac
Cramoisy

Réserve

Lac-des-
Champs

des

Lacs Albanal-

Lac
Champion

Lac
Cawachagamite

Mistassini-

MISCAU RÉSERVE

Rivière de Nemiscau

Lac des
Montagnes

Waconichi

4

Lac Woollett

Lac Bellinger

Rivière de Rupert

Rivière à la Marée

Lac
la Bordèliere

17 km   A   76°   95   B   75° Lac
Robineau   96   C   74°

Lac
Camousitchouane   Lac
Villon

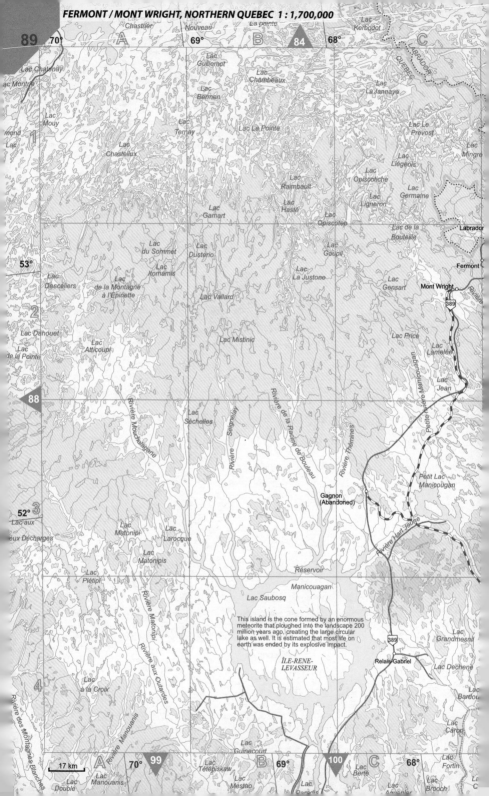

FERMONT / MONT WRIGHT, NORTHERN QUEBEC 1 : 1,700,000

84

Chastrier
Nouveau
La pointe
Lac
Kerbodot

LABRADOR

QUEBEC

70'
69°
68°

Lac Guillemot

Lac Chambeaux

Lac La Jannaye

Lac Chatenay

ac Montre

Lac Mouy

Lac Bermen

Lac Ternay

Lac La Pointe

Lac Le Prevost

Lac Mingre

mona Lac

Lac Chastellux

Lac Liégeois

Lac Opiscotiche

Lac Raimbault

Lac Germaine

Lac Ligneron

Lac Hasté

Lac Gamart

Lac Opiscoteo

Lac de la Bouteille

Labrador

Lac du Sommet

Lac Dusterio

Lac Goupil

53°

Lac Desceliers

Lac Itomamis

Lac de la Montagne à l'Epinette

Lac Vallard

Lac La Justone

Lac Gensart

Fermont

Mont Wright

389

Lac Dahouet

Lac de la Pointe

Lac Atticoupi

Lac Mistinic

Lac Price

Lac Lamelée

88

Lac Séchelles

Rivière Mouchalagane

Rivière Seignelay

Rivière de la Racine de Bouleau

Rivière Thémines

Petite Rivière Manicouagan

Lac Jean

Petit Lac Manicougan

Gagnon (Abandoned)

52°

Lac aux eux Décharges

Lac Matonipi

Lac Larocque

Rivière Hart-Jaune

Lac Matonipis

Réservoir

Lac Plétipi

Rivière Matonipi

Manicouagan

Lac Saubosq

Lac Grandmesnil

This island is the cone formed by an enormous meteorite that ploughed into the landscape 200 million years ago, creating the large circular lake as well. It is estimated that most life on earth was ended by its explosive impact.

389

Relais Gabriel

Lac Dechene

ÎLE-RENE-LEVASSEUR

Rivière aux Outardes

Lac à la Croix

Lac Bardou

Lac Carou

4

Rivière des Montagnes-Blanches

Lac Double

17 km

70°

Lac Manouanis

Lac Tétépiskaw

Lac Mesteo

69°

Lac Guinecourt

Lac Berté

68°

Lac Fortin

Lac Brooch

99
100

A
B
C

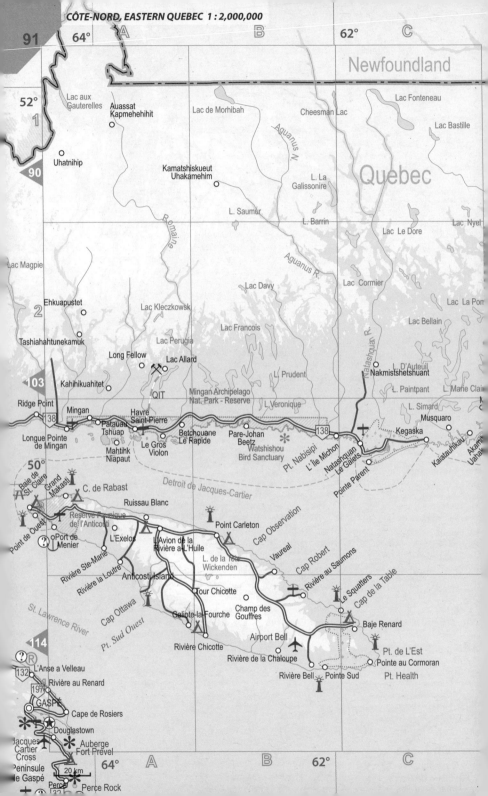

91
64°
A
B
62°
C

Newfoundland

52°
1

Lac aux Gauterelles

Auassat Kapmehehihit

Lac de Morhibah

Cheesman Lac

Lac Fonteneau

Lac Bastille

Quebec

90

Uhatnihip

Kamatshiskueut Uhakamehim

Aguanus N.

L. La Galissonire

L. Barrin

Lac Nyel

L. Saumur

Lac Le Dore

Romaine

Aguanus R.

Lac Davy

Lac Cormier

Lac La Pom

Lac Magpie

Ehkuapustet

Lac Kleczkowski

Lac Bellain

Nat ashquan R.

2

Tashiahahtunekamuk

Lac Francois

Lac Perugia

L. D'Auteuil

Long Fellow

Lac Allard

Nakmistshetshuant

L. Marie Clair

03

Kahihikuahitet

L. Prudent

L. Paintpant

QIT

L. Veronique

L. Simard

Ridge Point

138

Mingan

Mingan Archipelago Nat. Park - Reserve

Musquaro

Havre Saint-Pierre

138

Kegaska

Longue Pointe de Mingan

Patauau Tshuap

Betchouane Le Rapide

Parc-Johan Beetz

Pt. Nabisipi

L'île Michon

Natashquan Le Galets

Kaiatauhikau

Akami Uahat

Le Gros Violon

Mahtihk Niapaut

Watshishou Bird Sanctuary

Pointe Parent

50°

Baie de St. Claire

Grand Makasti

C. de Rabast

Detroit de Jacques-Cartier

Ruisseau Blanc

Point Carleton

Cap Observation

Reserve Faunique de l'Anticosti

L'Exelos

L'Avion de la Rivière au L'Huile

Cap Robert

Point de Ouest

Port de Menier

Vaureal

Rivière au Saumons

Le Squatters

Cap de la Table

Rivière Ste-Marie

Rivière la Loutre

L. de la reine Wickenden

St. Lawrence River

Anticosti Island

Tour Chicotte

Champ des Gouffres

Baie Renard

Cap Ottawa

Geliote-la-Fourche

114

Pt. Sud Ouest

Rivière Chicotte

Airport Bell

Pt. de L'Est

Pointe au Cormoran

132

L'Anse a Velleau

Rivière de la Chaloupe

Pt. Health

Rivière au Renard

Rivière Bell

Pointe Sud

197

GASPÉ

Cape de Rosiers

Douglastown

Jacques Cartier Cross

Auberge Fort Prevel

Peninsule de Gaspé

20 km

64°
A
B
62°
C

Percé

Perce Rock

132

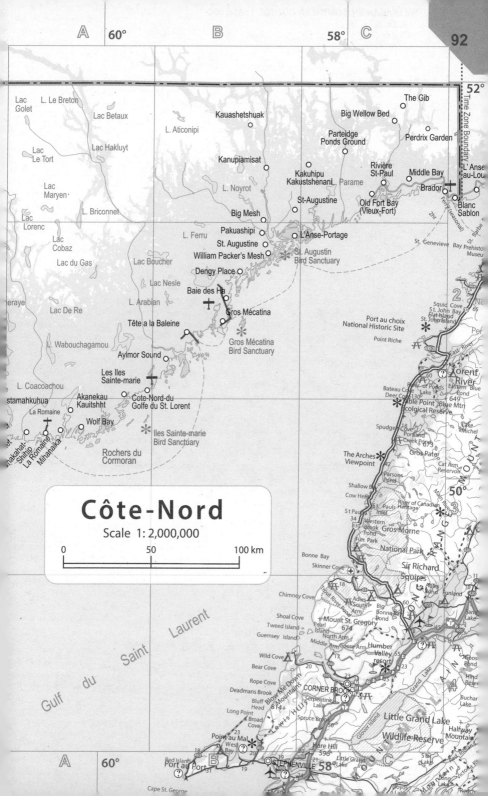

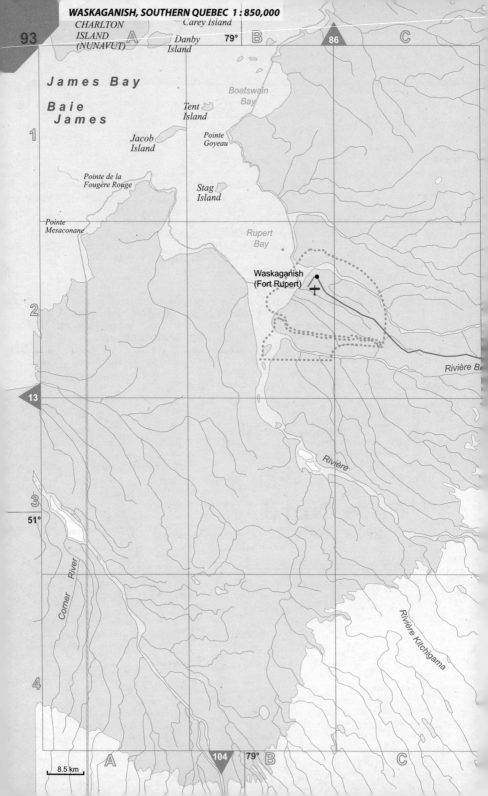

CHARLTON
ISLAND
(NUNAVUT)

Carey Island

Danby
Island

79°

A

B

86

C

James Bay

*Baie
James*

Boatswain
Bay

Tent
Island

Pointe
Goyeau

1

Jacob
Island

Pointe de la
Fougère Rouge

Stag
Island

Pointe
Mesaconane

Rupert
Bay

Waskaganish
(Fort Rupert)

2

13

Rivière B

Rivière

3

51°

Corner
River

Rivière Kitchigama

4

8.5 km

A

104

79°

B

C

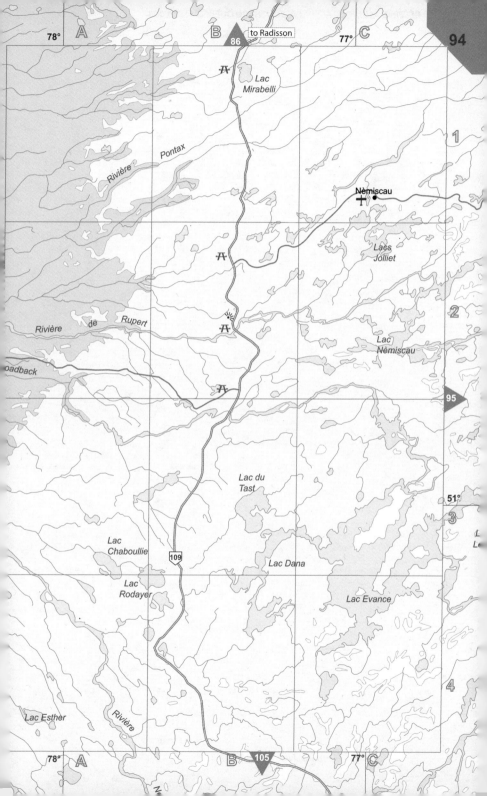

95

A 76° B 87 C

Lac
Cramoisy

Lac- des-
Champs

1

Lac
Champion

Rivière Nemiscau

Lac des
Montagnes

Rivière De Rupert

2

Rivière a la
Mattre

94

Lac
Legoff

Baie-James et
Eeyou Istchee

Lac
Tésècau

Lac
Camousitchouan

51°

3

Lac
Le Gardeur

Lac
Théodat

Lac
Deriares

Lac
Storm

Rivière Broadback

4

Lac
Caminscanane

Lac
Amisquioumisca 106 B 76° C

8.5 km

Lac
Mokachéa

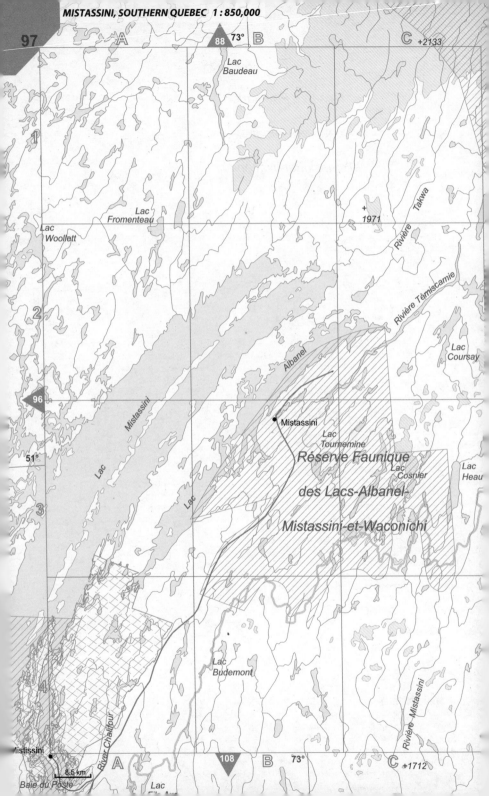

88 73°

+2133

Lac
Baudeau

Lac
Fromenteau

+
1971

Lac
Woollett

Rivière Takwa

Rivière Témiscamie

Albanel

Lac
Coursay

2

96

Mistassini

Lac
Mistassini

• Mistassini

Lac
Tournemine

Réserve Faunique

Lac
Cosnier

Lac
Heau

51°

des Lacs-Albanel-

Lac

3

Mistassini-et-Waconichi

Lac

Lac
Budemont

4

Rivière Mistassini

River Chalifour

Mistissini

8.5 km

Baie du Poste

108

73°

+1712

Lac

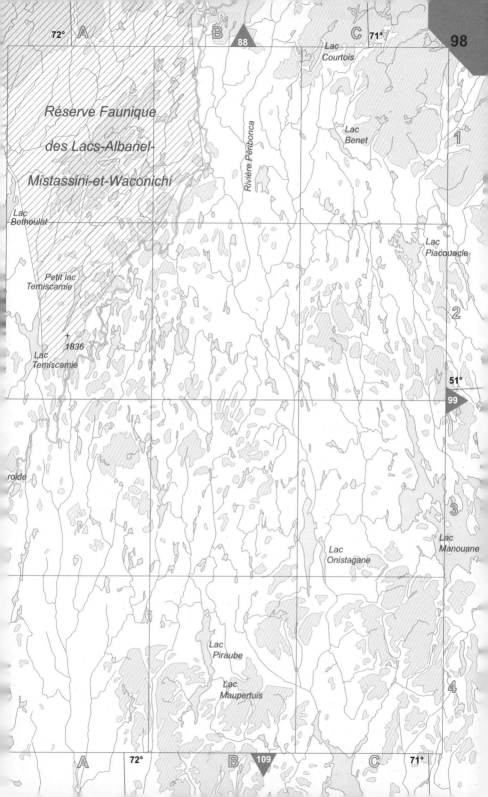

99

A

Lac
Plétipi

B 70° 89

Rivière Matonipi

C

1

Lac
A la Croix

Lac
Piacouacie

Lac
Tetepisk

2

2522+

Rivière Des Montagnes Blanches

Rivière Manuanis

+2769

51°

98

Lac
Manouanis

Lac
Double

Lac
Perdu

3

Lac
Manouane

Rivière Beisiamite

Rivière Presiin

4

Rivière Manouane

8.5 km

A

110

B

70°

C

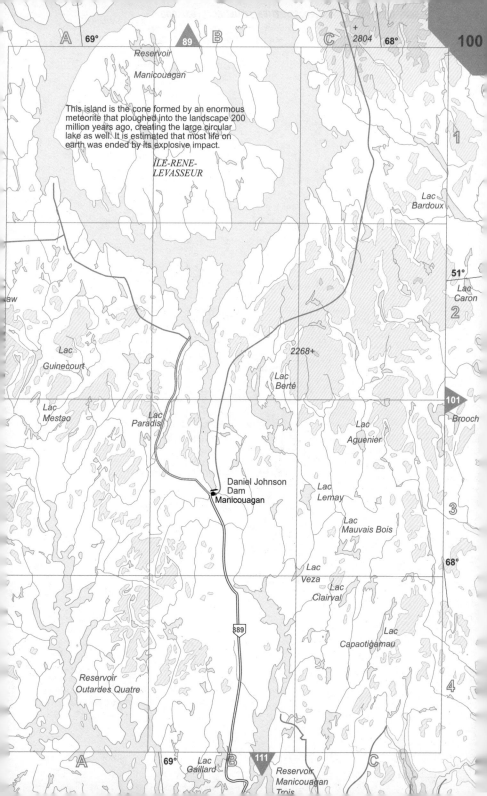

Reservoir
Manicouagan

This island is the cone formed by an enormous
meteorite that ploughed into the landscape 200
million years ago, creating the large circular
lake as well. It is estimated that most life on
earth was ended by its explosive impact.

ÎLE-RENE-
LEVASSEUR

+ 2804

Lac
Bardoux

51°

Lac
Caron

aw

Lac
Guinecourt

2268+

Lac
Berté

Lac
Mestao

Lac
Paradis

101

Brooch

Lac
Aguenier

Daniel Johnson
Dam
Manicouagan

Lac
Lemay

Lac
Mauvais Bois

68°

Lac
Veza

Lac
Clairval

Lac
Capaotigamau

Reservoir
Outardes Quatre

389

Reservoir
Manicouagan
Trois

Lac
Gaillard

89

1

2

3

4

A 66° B 90 C 65°

Lac à l'Aigle

Rivière Magpie Ouest

1

Premio

Lac Nipissis

2535 +

Lac Tortue

Lac Manitou

Rivière — Waccuno

2568+

Lac Nipisso

Tika

Lac Bigot

Rivière au Bouleau

2

65°

Rivière Moisie

Nicman

Lac des Eudistes

103

Rivière Sheldrake

Parc Provincial de Rivière Matamec

River Manitou

Rivière-aux-Graines

Manitou

138

R

3

Lac Matamec

Pointe St Charles

Baie de Moisie

Sept-îles

Maliotenam

Baie des Sept îles

Moisie

50°

La Grosse Boule

Gallix

nte-guerite

4

A 66° B 113 C

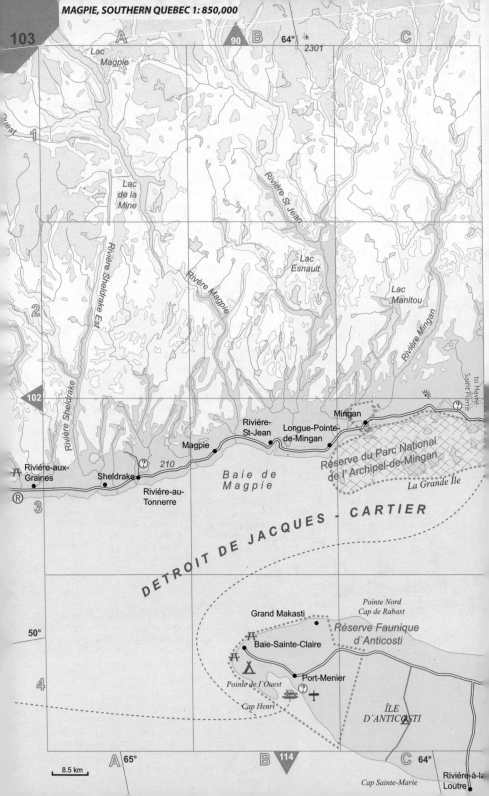

A
90 B
64°
2301
C

1

Lac
Magpie

Ouest

Lac
de la
Mine

Rivière Sheldrake Est

Rivière St Jean

2

Rivière Magpie

Lac
Esnault

Lac
Manitou

Rivière Mingan

to Havre-
Saint-Pierre

102

Rivière Sheldrake

Mingan

Rivière-
St-Jean

Longue-Pointe-
de-Mingan

Réserve du Parc National
de l' Archipel-de-Mingan

La Grande Île

Rivière-aux-
Graines

Sheldrake

Magpie

Baie de
Magpie

210

Rivière-au-
Tonnerre

R
3

DETROIT DE JACQUES - CARTIER

Pointe Nord
Cap de Rabast

Grand Makasti

Réserve Faunique
d`Anticosti

50°

Baie-Sainte-Claire

Port-Menier

4

Pointe de l`Ouest

Cap Henri

ÎLE
D`ANTICOSTI

A
65°

B
114

C
64°

Cap Sainte-Marie

Rivière-à-la-
Loutre

8.5 km

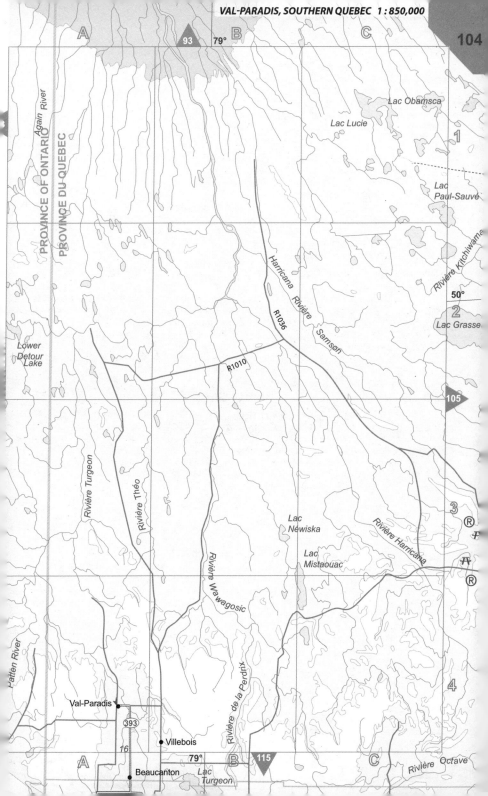

Lac Obamsca

Lac Lucie

Lac
Paul-Sauvé

Rivière Kitchiwame

Again River

PROVINCE OF ONTARIO

PROVINCE DU-QUEBEC

Harricana Rivière Samson

R1036

50°

Lac Grasse

R1010

Lower
Detour
Lake

Rivière Turgeon

Rivière Théo

Lac
Néwiska

Rivière Harricana

Rivière Wawagosic

Lac
Mistaouac

Patten River

Rivière de la Perdrix

Val-Paradis

393

16

Villebois

Beaucanton

Lac
Turgeon

79°

Rivière Octave

MATAGAMI SOUTHERN QUEBEC 1 : 850,000

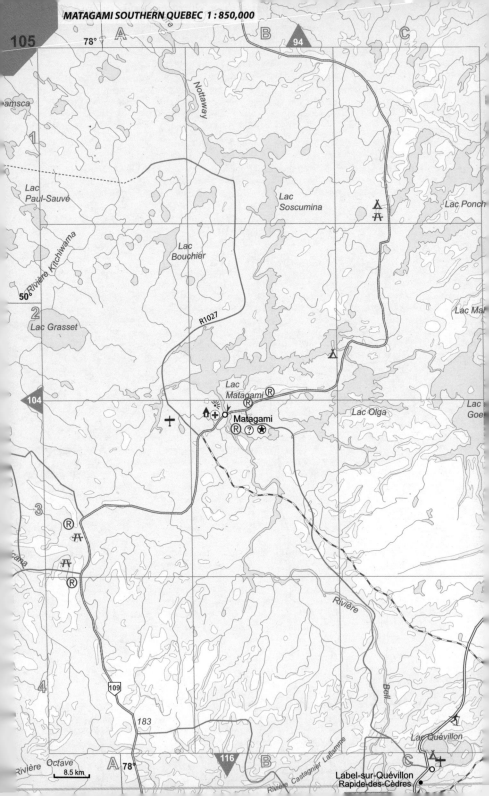

78°

A

B

94

C

1

amsca

Lac
Paul-Sauvé

Nottaway

Lac
Soscumina

Lac Ponch

50°

2

Rivière Kitchigama

Lac Grasset

Lac
Bouchier

R1027

Lac Mai

104

Lac
Matagami

R

R

Matagami

R

?

Lac Olga

Lac
Goe

Lac

3

R

cana

R

Rivière

4

109

183

Bell

Rivière Castagnier Laflamme

Lac Quévillon

A

78°

B

116

C

Octave
8.5 km

Rivière

Label-sur-Quévillon
Rapide-des-Cèdres

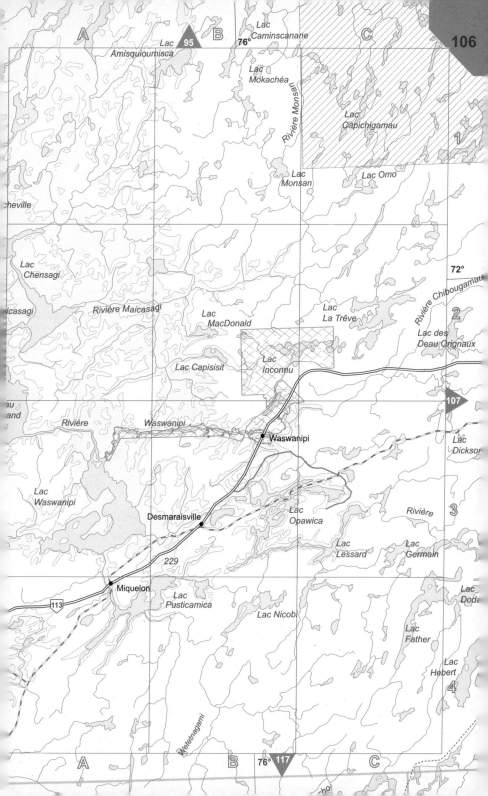

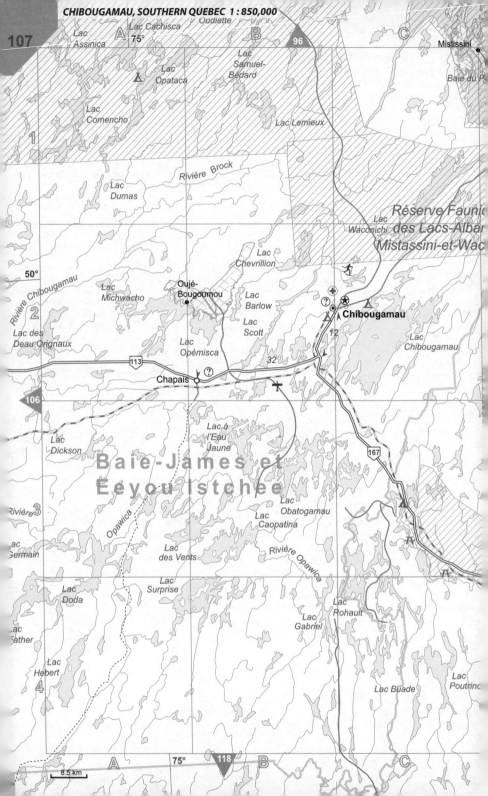

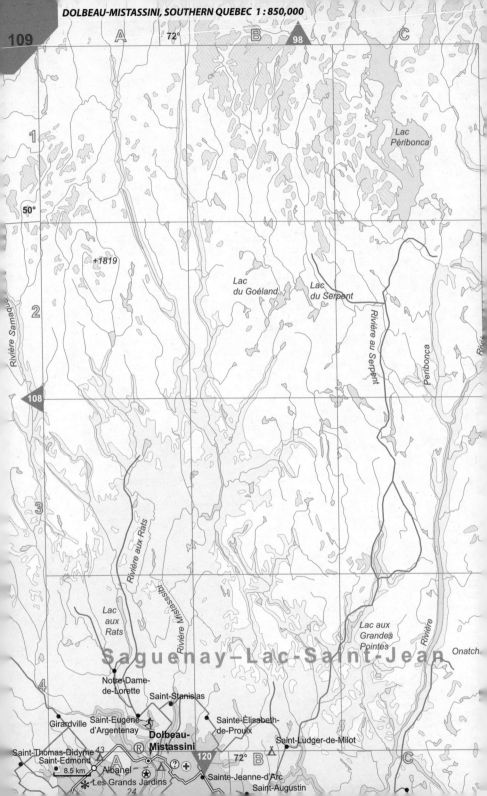

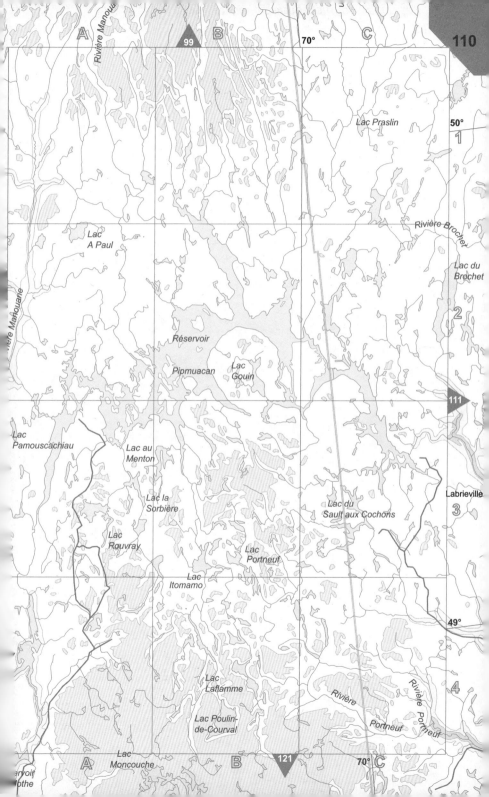

69°

100

Lac Gaillard

Reservoir Manicouagan Trois

50°

1

Lac Carteret

Rivière Brochet

Rivière aux Remous

Reservoir Manic Deux

Lac du Brochet

Rivière

110

2

Boucher

389

Lac au Loup-Marin

Rivière

Hauterive

Chute-aux-Outardes

Les Bui

Labrieville

3

Betsiamites

Ruisseau-Vert

Ragueneau

Pointe

PENINSU DE MAN

M a n i c o u a g a n

Papinachois

Betsiamites

385

Rivière-Bersimis

Pointe Betsiamites

Rivière du Sault

100

aux Cochons

Saint-Marc-de-Latour

Ⓡ

Cap Colombier

Rivière Portneuf

4

✝

?

Pointe Orient

Forestville

112

A

B

69°

C

8.5 km

Sainte-Anne-de-Portneuf

Sainte

68° A B 67° C

101

1

Lac Pentecôte

La Tete de Chien

Baie des Hoamrds

Rivière-Pentecôte

Pointe-aux-Anglais

Riviére Godbout

138

Lac Doinne

Les Islets-Caribou

2

Baie-Trinité

ac La hesnaye

Lac de Monts

Phare de Pointe-des-Monts

Franquelin Godbout

113

Pointe a la Croix

FLEUVE SAINT - LAURENT RIVER

Baie-Comeau

Capucins

49°

Pointe-Label

Les Méchins

ns

Pointe Paradis

3

x-Outardes

OUAGAN

132

Grosses-Roches

L'Anse-à-la-Croix

Ste-Félicité

Fish market

St Jean de Cherbourg

Mont Blanc

Matàne

Petite-Matane

Saint-Adelme

St-Ulric

Saint-Luc

Réserve Matane

132

65

St-René-de-Matane

Baie-des-Sables

195

Les Boules

Saint-Leandre

65

Rivière Matane

MONTS CHIC-CHOCS

4

Jardins de Métis

Métis-sur-Mer

Saint-Damase

Sainte-Paule

297

Saint-Vianney

Grand-Métis

St-Noël

Saint-Tharcisius

67°

ainte-Flavie

Price

Sayabec

Lac Matapédia

123

Mont-Joli

Saint-Octave

Padoue

Lac Casault

Saint-Alexandre-des-Lacs

de-Métis

Saint-Joseph

68°   75

St-Moise

Val-Brillant

Saint-Cléophas

132

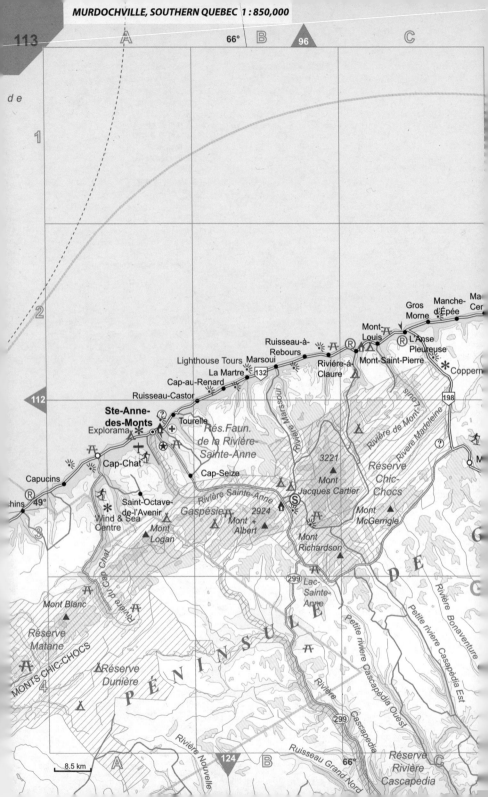

113   A   66°   B   96   C

de

1

2

112

49°

3

A   66°   B   124   C

MURDOCHVILLE, SOUTHERN QUEBEC 1 : 850,000

Ma-
Cer
Manche-
d'Épée
Gros
Morne
Mont-
Louis
L'Anse
Pleureuse
Coppern
Ruisseau-à-
Rebours
Mont-Saint-Pierre
Lighthouse Tours   Marsoui
La Martre   132
Rivière-à-
Claure
Cap-au-Renard
Ruisseau-Castor
**Ste-Anne-
des-Monts**
Explorama
Tourelle
*Rés.Faun.
de la Rivière-
Sainte-Anne*
198
Capucins
Cap-Chat
Cap-Seize
3221
*Mont
Jacques Cartier*
*Réserve
Chic-
Chocs*
Saint-Octave-
de-l'Avenir
Rivière Sainte-Anne
Gaspésie
2924
*Mont
Albert*
*Mont
McGerrigle*
Wind & Sea
Centre
*Mont
Logan*
*Mont
Richardson*
Mont Blanc
299   *Lac-
Sainte-
Anne*
*Réserve
Matane*
*Réserve
Dunière*
MONTS CHIC-CHOCS
PÉNINSULE
DE
299
Rivière Bonaventure
Petite rivière Casapédia Est
Petite rivière Casapédia Ouest
*Rivière
Cascapédia*
Ruisseau Grand Nord
Rivière Nouvelle
*Réserve
Rivière
Cascapedia*

8.5 km

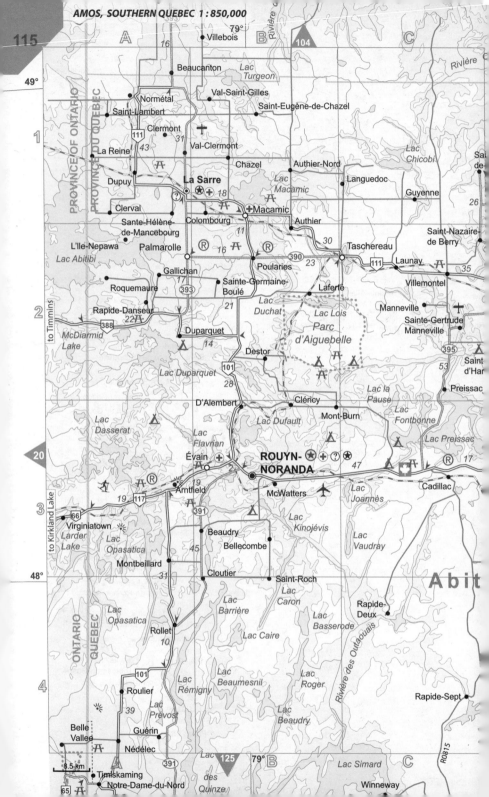

115

49°

79°

A   B   104   C

Villebois

Rivière

Lac Turgeon

Beaucanton

Val-Saint-Gilles

Normétal   Saint-Eugène-de-Chazel

Saint-Lambert

1   Clermont   31   Val-Clermont

111   43

La Reine   Chazel   Authier-Nord   Languedoc   Lac Chicobi   Sai de—

Dupuy   La Sarre   18   Lac Macamic   Guyenne

?   ⊛ ✛   26

Clerval   Macamic   Authier

Sante-Hélène-   Colombourg   Saint-Nazaire-
de-Mancebourg   11   de Berry

L'Ile-Nepawa   Palmarolle   ® 16   ®   390   23   Tascherau   111   Launay   35

Lac Abitibi   Poularies   30   Villemontel

Gallichan   17   Sainte-Germaine-   Laferté   Manneville   395
Roquemaure   393   Boulé   Lac   Sainte-Gertrude   Saint
21   Duchat   Lac Lois   Manneville   d'Har

Rapide-Danseur   22   Parc   53
388   Duparquet   14   d'Aiguebelle   Preissac

McDiarmid   Destor   Lac la
Lake   101   Pause

Lac Duparquet   28   Cléricy   Lac   Lac Preissac
Fontbonne

D'Alembert   Mont-Burn

Lac   Lac Dufault
Dasserat   Lac
Flavrian   17

20   Évain   ⊕   ROUYN-   47   Cadillac
NORANDA   ⊛ ⊕ ? ⊛   ✛

3   19   Arntfield   McWatters   ✈   Lac
117   391   Joannès

to Kirkland Lake   66   Lac   Lac
Virginiatown   Opasatica   Beaudry   Kinojévis   Lac
Larder   45   Bellecombe   Vaudray
Lake   Montbeillard
31   Cloutier   Saint-Roch

48°   Lac
Caron
Lac   Rapide-
Barrière   Lac   Deux
Lac   Basserode
Opasatica   Rollet
10   Lac Caire   A b i t

101   Lac   Lac
4   Roulier   Rémigny   Roger   Rapide-Sept
39   Lac
Prévost
Belle   Guérin   Lac
Vallée   Beaudry
8.5 km   Nédélec
391   Lac   125   79°   Lac Simard   C
65   Timiskaming   des
Notre-Dame-du-Nord   Quinze   Winneway

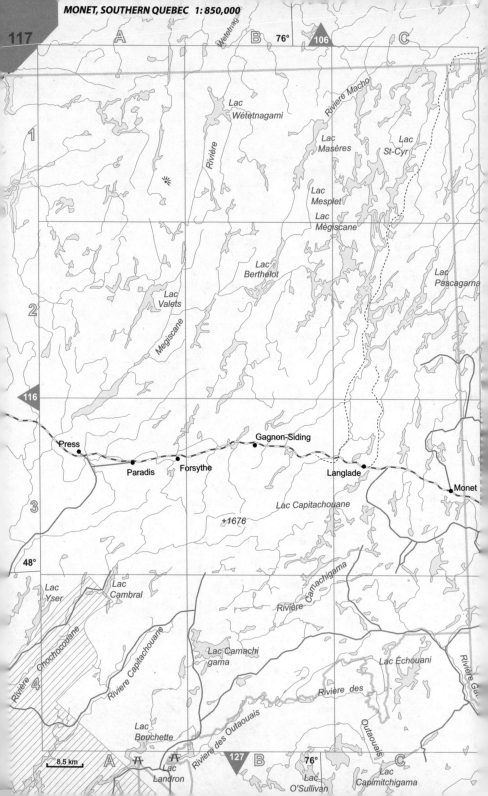

MONET, SOUTHERN QUEBEC 1:850,000

A   B   76°   106   C

Wetetnag

1

Lac
Wétetnagami

Rivière

Rivière Macho

Lac
Masères

Lac
St-Cyr

Lac
Mesplet

Lac
Mégiscane

Lac
Berthelot

Lac
Pascagarna

2

Lac
Valets

Mégiscane

116

Press

Gagnon-Siding

Paradis   Forsythe

Langlade

Monet

3

Lac Capitachouane

+1676

48°

Lac
Yser

Lac
Cambral

Rivière Camachigama

Lac Échouani

Rivière Ga

Rivière Chochocouane

Rivière Capitachouane

Lac Camachi
gama

Rivière   des

Outaouais

4

Lac
Bouchette

Rivière des Outaouais

8.5 km

A   127   B   76°   C

Lac
Landron

Lac
O'Sullivan

Lac
Capimitchigama

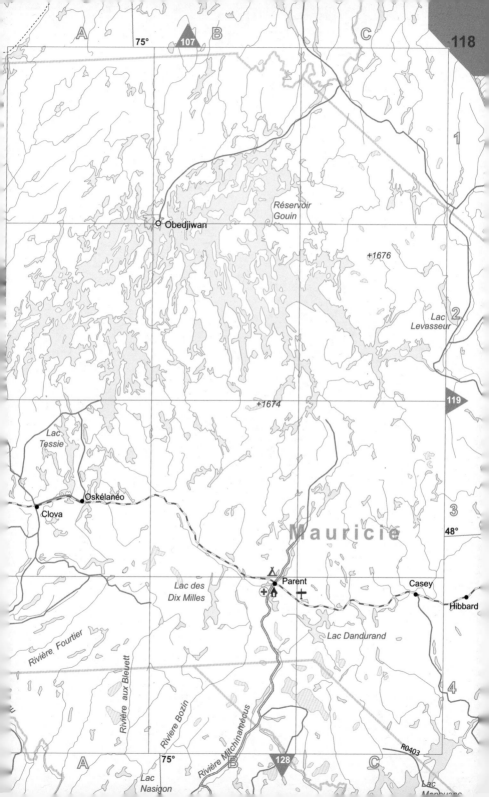

A 113 B 299 66° Cascapédia Ouest C

Rivière Nouvelle
Ruisseau Grand Nord

Réserve
Rivière
Cascapédia

Grande-
Cascapédia

Saint-Jules Saint-Edgar English Colonia
Architecture

Rivière Escuminac

Gesgapegiag 132 New Richmond Saint-Alphonse

jaw Sainte-Marguerite Maria Black Cape Caplan

Rivière Kempt Rivière Assemetquagan

Nouvelle 70 Baie
de
Cascapédia

L'Alverne Escuminac 132 Saint-Omer ?

Pointe-à- Drapeau ?
la-Garde Restigouche

Saint-André- Miguasha Carleton
de-Restigouche

Oak Dalhousie 48°
Bay

Pointe-à- QUEBEC
la-Croix NEW BRUNSWICK

Charlo

ttlement Listuguj Eel River Jacquet Belledune
Crossing River

Matapédia Atholville Pte Verte

Saint-Alexis- Bataille-de-la- Sugarloaf 11
e-Matapédia Restigouche Charlo River Benjamin River
Dawsonville South Chato River 2

WICK

neval Upsalquitch River S Branch Benjamin R Nigadoo
Berestord

NEW BRUNSWICK Bathurst

Boland Brook

rook 3

114 Réserve
Port-Daniel Pabos Mills

124 Newport

Bonaventure River 132 Pointe au Maquereau

English Colonial Clemville L'Anse-aux- Gascons
Architecture Port-Daniel-Gascons 48°

Saint-Alphonse Saint-Jogues Marcil 175

Saint-Elzéar Kelly Shigawake

Acadian Caplan Church Rivière- Saint-Godefroi
Paspébiac Hope Town

Caplan Bonaventure Paspébiac Wa

St-Siméon New Carlisle 47°

CHALEUR BAY 65° 4

385 A 67° B C 66° Red Bar

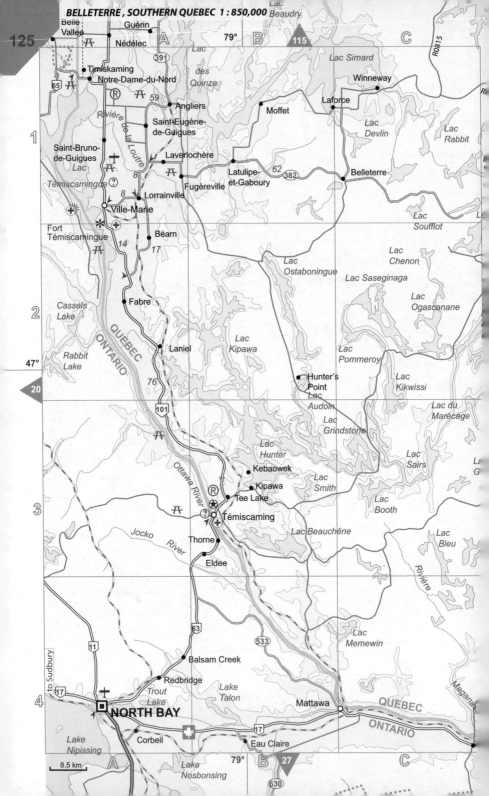

A

B

117

76°

Outaouais

C

Lac Bouchette

Rivière des Outaouais

Lac Landron

Lac O'Sullivan

Lac Capimitchigama

1

Rivière Bélinge

Lac McLennan

Rivière du

Réservoir Cabonga

Lac Maxime

Lac Séguin

Lac Saint-Amour

Lac Lecoir

221

Lac Rapide

Lac Camatose

Lac Poigan

2

Lac Grand

47°

Lac Byrd

Lac Jean-Péré

Lac de L'Ecorce

Rivière Gens de Terre

Lac Antostagnau

Rivière Notawas

126

Lac Kondiaronk

Lac Embarras

Lac Delahey

Réservoir Baskatong

Lac Gale

Lac Gagamo

Ferme-

3

Lac Doolittle

117

Grand-Remous

Lac Barton

?

Val-Limoges

Lac Désert

Montcerf

Ⓡ

13

Saint-Jean-sur-le-Lac

30

Lac-Gatineau

Lac Brodikorb

Bois-Franc

X 17

105

Saint-Cajetan

Lac David

41

107

Lac Quinn

Lac Bryson

Lac à la Tortue

?

Sainte-Famille d'Aumond

des

Rivière Gatineau

Lac Pythonga

Lac des Abattis

?

Déléage

4

Maniwaki

✚

✴

Sainte-Thérèse-de-la-Gatineau

Notre-D-de-Pon

Lac Duval

Rivière de l'Aigle

Lac des Cèdres

Messines

Farley

Lac des Trente et Un Milles

Lac (Re

8.5 km

Lac Mer Bleue

Lac Blue Sea

Bouchette

134

Blue Sea

57

?

Lac

A

B

C

Lac Galarneau

Lac-Cayamant

Gracefield

Notre-

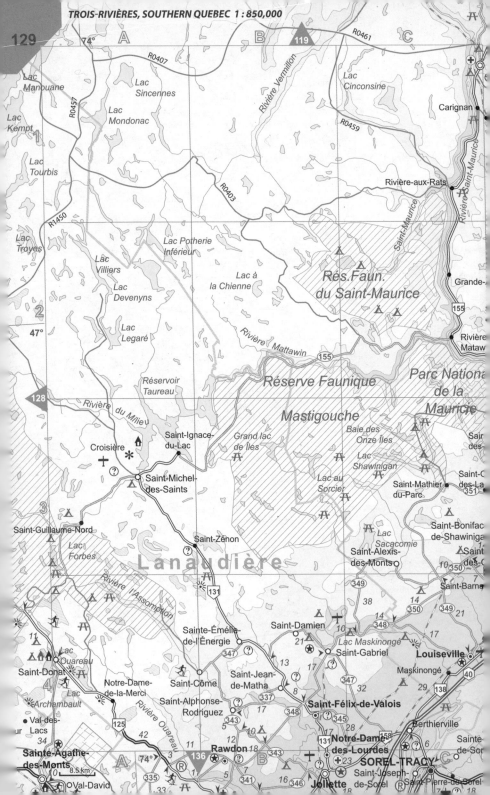

131

Saint-Bernard-sur-Mer
La Baleine
Saint-Placide-de-Charlevoix
Saint-Cassien-des-Caps
Saint-Louis-de-l'Isle-aux-Coudres
Île Aux Coudres
Village-des-Aulnaies
C
19
La

Mont Raoul-Blanchard
Forêt Montmorency
Rivière Montmorency
Rivière Sainte-Anne
138
Petite-Rivière-Saint-François
Saint-Roch-des-Aulnaies
Windmill
Saint-Jean-Port-Joli
132
Saint-Dam-des-Aulnai
Saint

Parc de la Jacques-Cartier
Windmill
Trois-Saumons
Saint-Aubert
20

Saint-Ferréol-les-Neiges
360
L'Islet-sur-Mer
13
L'Islet
Wood Museum
Sainte-
39

Famous pilgrimage church
Beaupré
Cap-St-Ignace
13
132
Saint-Eugène
Saint-Cyrille-de-l
34
Sain

Sainte-Anne-de-Beaupré
FLEUVE ST-LAURENT
Maritime Museum

Tewesbury
175
Château-Richer
25
368
ÎLE D'ORLÉANS
60
Montmagny
Geese watching
Bras-d'Apic
285

371
47°
41
Boischatel
Saint-Pierre
Saint-Michel-de-Bellechasse
37
Saint-Francois Montmagny
283
Notre-Dame-du-Rosaire
25
Sainte-

Shannon
24
Lorette Ville
19
228
25
31
Saint-Paul-de-Montminy
283
Saint-Fabien-de-Panet
7

Val-Bélair
L'Ancienne-Lorette
BEAUPORT
CHARLESBOURG
Beaumont
218
13
Carriage Museum
33
281
Saint-Philémon
9
Sainte-L
de-Beau
Sainte-L
19

Cap-Rouge
LÉVIS
QUÉBEC
SAINTE-FOY
Saint-Romuald
11
Saint-Charles-de-Bellechasse
281
Gold Rush
28
Saint Magloire
Saint-Just-Bretenière
281

Justin-
aures
Saint-Nicolas
Saint-Jean-Chrysostome
Saint-Henri
279
Saint-Anselme
39
Sainte-Claire
11
Siant-Damien-de-Buckland
19
216
Sainte-Sabine
Sai
de-

Charny
218
173
277
29
14
275
7
5
12
5
Saint-Édouard-de-Frampton
Lac-Etchemin
Saint-Léon-de-Standon
24
Sainte-Sab
Station

Saint-Apollinaire
13
273
Saint-Agapit
Saint-Gilles
15
17
171
73
9
10
216
5
112
13
Sainte-Justine

130
11
18
Dosquet
12
Sainte-Marie
14
15
275
Saint-Odilon
Sainte-Cyprien

Lyster
3
16
271
218
20
269
25
Vallée-Jonction
9
73
20
276
275
Saint-Louis-de-Gonzague
277
19

Laurierville
267
36
Saint-Jacques-de-Leeds
Tring-Jonction
12
8
73
14
Saint-Joseph-de-Beauce
29
Beauceville
Saint-Prosper
15
12

Inverness
11
271
112
East Broughton
108
25
204
173
Sainte-Auréli

24
216
11
269
20
269
15
6
1
Robertsonville
Miniature Village
Saint-Benoît-Labre
271
Saint-Georges
12
275
19
Saint-Zacharie
Antique Car Museum

Saint-Ferdinand
166
14
8
Thetford Mines
Black Lake
16
269
11
Saint-Ephrem-de-Beauce
27
Saint-Côme Linière
Saint-Martin
15
Armstrong
Lac du Por
St
Théophile

19
24
267
Adstock
Mine Tours
La Guadeloupe
21
269
16
269

8.5 km
Disraëli
27
Lac Saint-Franç
ois
19
138
71
B
9
173
C
14
Saint-Gédéon-

21

Saint-Pacôme 287

à Pocatière

Saint-Gabriel-Lalemant

Saint-
Onésime
d'Ixworth

nte-Louise

mase-
aies

Rivière Ouelle

Lac
Sainte-Anne

CANADA

UNITED STATES

122

B

Little Black

69°

C

Saint-François-
de-Madawaska

Corthers

132

204

Tourville

Saint-Omer

161

Allagash

St John River

Eagle
Lake

1

47°

Perpetue

l'Islet

204

10

?

Saint-Pamphile

Allagash River

Fish River
Lake

nte-Félicité

216

22

23

Saint-Marce

Saint-Adalbert

22

U N I T E D   S T A T E S

First Musquacook
Lake

2

polline

13

204

Long Lake

19

ucie-
egard

3

19

283

Clayton
Lake

Chemquasabamticook
Lake

Churchill
Lake

Pleasent
Lake

quam

e-

17

Eagle
Lake

Camille-
llis

ne-

QUEBEC

MAINE

Allagash
Lake

Chamberlain
Lake

Grand
Lake
Matagamon

3

Black Pond

Chesuncook

46°

+4077
Mnt. Katahdin

4

Lake

70°

A

Moosehead Lake

Big Spence Mnt.
+2502

B

C

69°

Pemadumcook
Lake

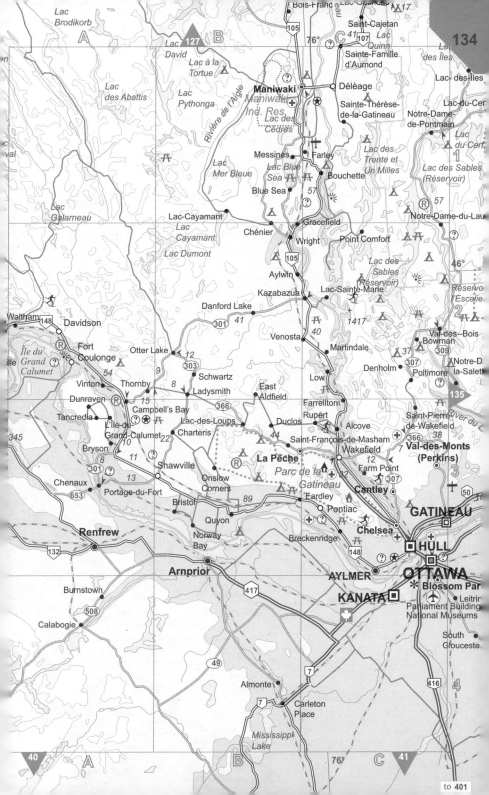

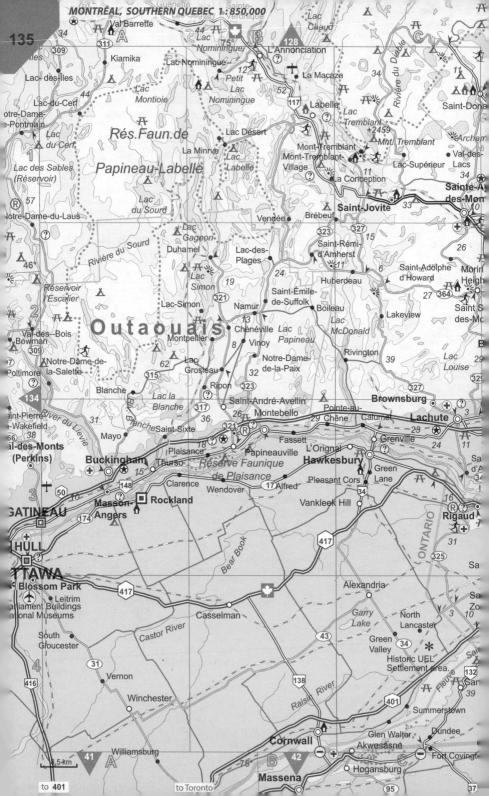

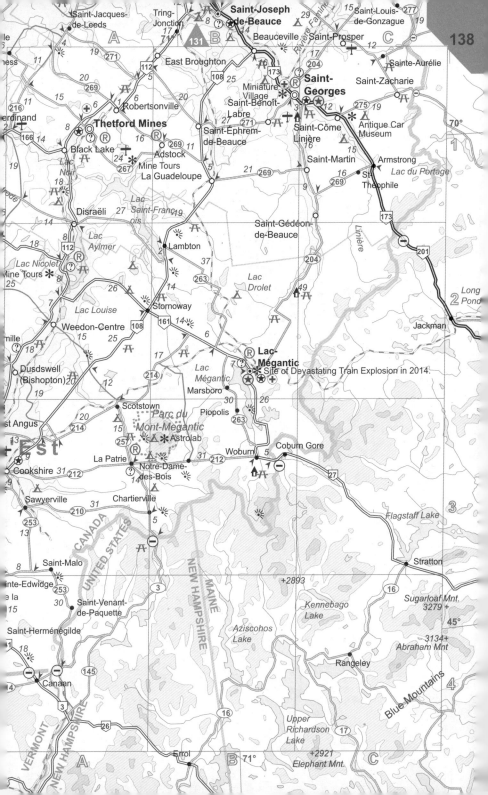

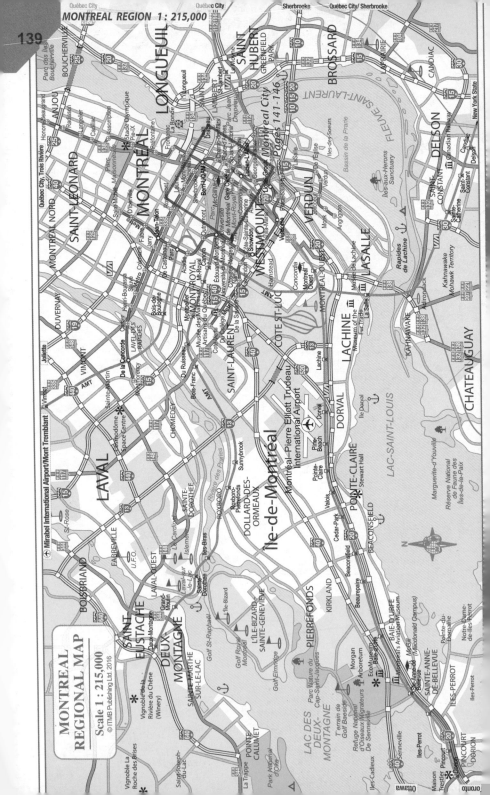

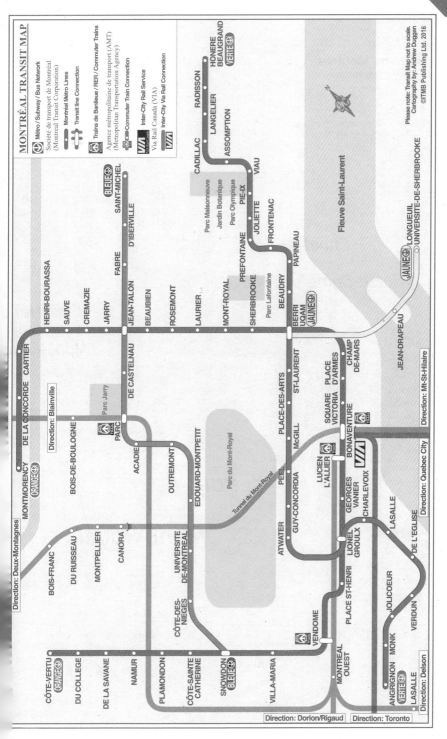

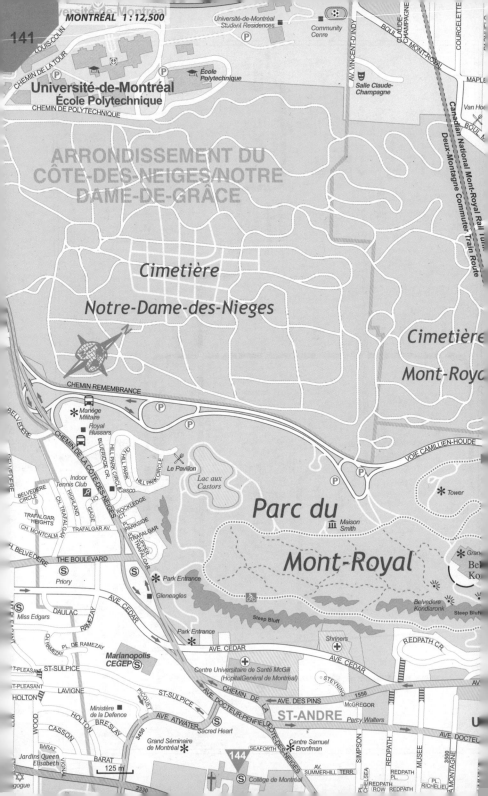

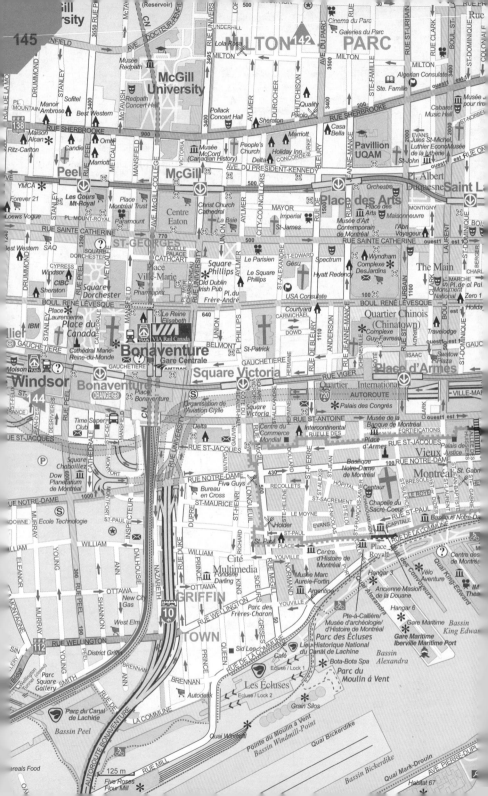

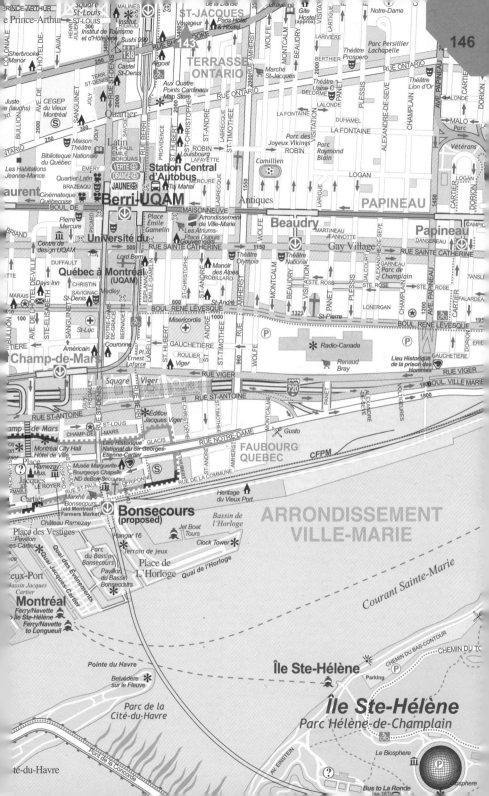

INDEX

Aberfoyle 53-A4
Achigan......................21-B2
Actinolite...................49-A1
Acton 53-B3
Acton Vale..................137-A2
Adams Ctr..................50-C3
Addison.....................41-C4
Adelaide....................56-A3
Adolphustown...............49-C3
Adstock.....................131-B4
Agawa Bay..................18-B4
Ahmic Harbour..............36-C3
Ailsa Craig.................56-A3
Ajax........................54-B2
Akamiht Uahakutet..........91-C3
Akanekau Kauitshht.........92-A2
Akron.......................59-C1
Akulivik....................79-A3
Akwesasne..................135-C4
Alban.......................35-B2
Albanel.....................120-A1
Albertville.................123-C1
Alburg......................136-C4
Alcona......................46-B4
Alcove......................31-A3
Alcove......................134-C3
Aldershot...................58-A1
Alexandria..................32-C4
Alexandria..................135-C4
Alexandria Bay.............50-C1
Alfred......................32-B3
Alfred......................135-B3
Algoma Mills...............33-A3
Algoma Mills...............22-C4
Algonac.....................61-A1
Algonquin...................41-C3
Alice.......................29-B4
Allagash....................132-C1
Allan Park..................52-A2
Allenford...................51-B1
Alliston....................53-B1
Alma........................52-C3
Alma........................120-B1
Almont......................60-B1
Almonte.....................41-A2
Almonte.....................134-B4
Alton.......................53-A3
Alvanley....................44-B4
Alvinston...................55-C4
Amberley....................51-A3
Ameliasburg................49-A4
Amesdale...................14-C1
Amherst.....................59-B1
Amherstburg................60-C4
Amherstview................49-C2
Amos........................116-A2
Amqui.......................123-B1
Amulree.....................56-C1
Amyot.......................18-A3
Ancaster....................57-C1
Anchorville.................60-C1
Andy' Corners..............57-B3
Angle Inlet.................14-A2
Angle Inlet.................14-A3
Angliers....................20-B3
Angliers....................125-A1
Angola......................59-B2
Angus.......................46-A4
Annan.......................45-A4
Anten Mills.................46-A4
Antrim......................41-B1
Appin.......................56-A4
Apple Hill..................32-C4

Apsley......................48-A1
Apto........................46-A4
Arbor-Vitae.................14-B3
Ardbeg......................36-B3
Arden.......................40-B4
Ardtrea.....................46-C3
Argyle......................47-A3
Ariss.......................52-C4
Arkona......................55-C3
Armstrong...................10-B4
Armstrong...................131-C4
Arnesen.....................14-A3
Arnprior....................40-C1
Arnprior....................134-B3
Arnstein....................36-B2
Arntfield...................115-A3
Aroland.....................11-A4
Arpoch......................40-A3
Arthur......................52-C3
Arva........................56-B3
Asbestos....................137-C2
Ascot Corner...............137-C3
Ash Lake....................15-A4
Ashford Hollow.............59-C3
Ashton......................41-A2
Ashuanipi...................90-B2
Astorville..................27-A4
Astray......................84-C3
Athens......................41-B4
Atherley....................46-C3
Atholville..................124-A2
Atikokan....................15-B3
Attawapiskat................7-B3
Atwood......................52-A4
Auassat Kapmehehihit.......91-A1
Auburn......................51-B4
Auclair.....................122-C3
Auden.......................10-C4
Aupaluk.....................78-C1
Aurora......................53-C2
Austin......................137-B4
Authier.....................20-B1
Authier-Nord...............115-B1
Avening.....................53-A1
Avon........................57-A3
Avonmore...................42-B1
Ayer's Cliff...............137-C4
Aylmer......................57-A4
AYLMER......................134-C3
Aylmor Sound...............92-A2
Aylwin......................30-C2
Aylwin......................134-B2
Ayr.........................57-B1
Ayton.......................52-A2
Azilda......................25-A4
Baddow......................47-B2
Baden.......................57-A1
Badjeros....................52-C1
Baie de St. Claire.........91-A3
Baie des Ha................92-B2
Baie-Comeau................112-A3
Baie-des- Sables...........112-A4
Baie-des-Bacon.............122-B1
Baie-des-Rochers...........122-A3
Baie-du-Febvre.............130-A4
Baie-Sainte- Catherine.....122-A2
Baie-Sainte-Claire.........103-B4
Baie-Saint-Paul............121-B4
Baie-Trinité...............112-C2
Baileboro...................48-A4
Baje Renard.................91-C4
Bala........................46-A1
Balaclava...................40-A2
Balderson...................41-A3
Baldwin.....................46-C4
Ballantrae..................54-A1
Ballymote...................56-B3

Balm Beach.................45-C3
Balmerton...................8-B4
Balmy Beach................44-C4
Balsam......................54-B1
Balsam Creek...............20-C4
Balsam Creek...............27-A3
Balsam Creek...............125-A4
Bamberg.....................57-A1
Bancroft....................39-A4
Bannockburn................48-B1
Baptiste....................39-A4
Barachois...................114-C3
Barbeau.....................21-B3
Barbers Bay................19-C2
Barclay.....................46-B4
Barkway.....................46-C2
Barnston....................137-C4
Barraute....................116-B2
Barrie......................46-B4
Barriefield.................50-A2
Barrow Bay..................44-B3
Barry's Bay................39-A2
Barry's Bay................133-B3
Barryvale...................40-B2
Barville....................116-B2
Barwick.....................14-B4
Batawa......................48-C3
Batchawana Bay.............21-A2
Batchawana Mountain........21-B1
Batchawana.................21-A2
Bath........................49-C3
Battersea...................50-A1
Baudette....................14-B4
Bayfield....................55-C1
Bayfield Inlet.............35-C3
Bayshore Village...........46-C3
Baysville...................37-C4
Beachburg...................30-A4
Beachville..................56-C2
Bealton.....................57-C2
Beamsville..................58-B1
Bear Island.................26-A2
Bear Lake...................37-A3
Beardmore...................16-C1
Beaucanton.................115-A1
Beaucarton.................20-A1
Beauceville................131-B4
Beaudry.....................20-B2
Beaudry.....................115-B3
Beauharnois................136-A4
Beaumont....................131-A2
BEAUPORT....................131-A2
Beaupré.....................131-B1
Beaverton...................47-A4
Bécancour...................130-B4
Bedford.....................137-A4
Beeton......................53-B1
Bégin.......................120-C1
Belcourt....................116-B2
Belgrave....................51-B4
Belle River.................61-A3
Belle Vallee...............115-A4
Belle Vallée...............20-B3
Belle-Anse.................114-C3
Bellecombe.................115-B3
Belledune...................124-C2
Bellefeuille...............135-C2
Belleterre.................125-C1
Belleville..................49-A3
Belleville..................60-A4
Belmont.....................56-C3
Belmore.....................51-C3
Beloeil.....................136-C3
Belwood.....................52-C3
Benny.......................19-B4
Benny.......................19-C4
Benny.......................24-A3

Beresford...................124-C2
Bergland....................14-B3
Berkeley....................52-A1
Berthierville...............129-C4
Bertram.....................18-A1
Bervie......................51-B2
Berwick.....................42-A1
Betchouane Le Rapide.......91-B3
Bethany.....................47-C4
Betsiamites................111-C4
Bewdley.....................48-A4
Biencourt...................122-C2
Big Bay.....................44-C3
Big Bay Point..............46-B4
Big Falls...................14-B4
Big Mesh....................92-B1
Big Wellow Bed.............92-C1
Billington Heights.........59-C2
Binbrook....................58-A1
Birch Island...............34-B2
Birchdale...................14-B4
Birds Creek.................39-A3
Birmingham.................60-A2
Birr........................56-B2
Biscotasing................23-B2
Bishops Mills..............41-C3
Bishopsgate................57-B2
Bismarck....................58-C1
Bissett Creek..............28-B3
Bissett Creek..............133-A2
Black Bay...................29-B4
Black Brook................123-C4
Black Cape.................124-C1
Black Donald...............40-A2
Black Hawk.................14-B3
Black Lake.................131-A4
Blackburn...................31-B4
Blacks Corners.............41-A2
Blackstock..................54-B1
Blackwater..................47-A4
Blainville.................136-A2
Blakeney....................41-B1
Blanc Sablon...............92-C1
Blanche.....................31-C3
Blanche.....................135-A2
Blenheim....................61-C2
Blezard Valley.............24-C4
Blind River................22-B4
Blind River................33-A3
Blomingdale................52-C4
Blossom Park...............41-C1
Blossom Park...............134-C4
Blue Sea....................30-B2
Blue Sea...................134-B2
Bluevale....................51-C3
Bluewater Beach............45-C3
Blyth.......................51-C4
Blytheswood................61-B4
Bobcaygeon.................47-B2
Bognor......................45-A4
Boileau.....................32-B2
Boileau....................135-B2
Boisbriand.................136-A3
Boischatel.................131-A2
Bois-Franc.................127-B3
Bolton......................53-B2
Bolton Centre..............137-B4
Bombay......................42-C1
Bon Echo...................40-A4
Bonarlaw....................48-C2
Bond Head..................53-B1
Bonfield....................27-B4
Bonville....................42-B1
Border......................14-B4
Bornholm....................56-B1
Boston......................57-C2
BAoucherville..............136-B3
Bouchette..................30-C1
Bouchette..................127-C4

Bougainville ...114-C3	C.F.B Borden ...53-A1	Cartier ...24-A4	Clarence ...32-A3
Boulter ...39-B3	C.F.B. North Bay ...20-B4	Casey ...118-C4	Clarence ...135-A3
Bourget ...32-A4	C.F.B. Kingston ...50-A2	Casselman ...32-A4	Clarence Creek ...31-C3
Bowman ...31-A2	C.F.B. North Bay ...26-C3	Casselman ...135-B4	Clarendon Station ...40-B4
Bowman ...134-C2	Cabano ...122-C3	Castleford ...40-B1	Clarina ...48-A2
Bowmanville ...54-C1	Cache Bay ...26-A4	Cat Lake ...9-A3	Clarke City ...101-C4
Boyne ...53-B4	Cacouna ...122-A3	Cataract ...53-A3	Clarke's Corners ...44-A2
Bracebridge ...46-B1	Cadillac ...115-C3	Catchacoma ...47-C2	Clarksburg ...45-B4
Bradford ...53-B1	Caesarea ...47-B4	Cathcart ...57-B2	Clarkson ...53-C4
Brador ...92-C1	Cairngorm ...56-A4	Causapscal ...123-C1	Clavering ...44-C4
Braeside ...40-B1	Cairo ...61-C1	Cavan ...47-C4	Clayton ...40-C2
Brampton ...53-B3	Caistor Centre ...58-B1	Cayuga ...58-A2	Clayton ...50-B2
Brantford ...57-C2	Caistorville ...58-B2	Cedar Beach ...61-A4	Clayton Lake ...132-B2
Bras-d'Apic ...131-C2	Calabogie ...40-B2	Cedar Mills ...53-B2	Clear Creek ...57-B4
Brebeuf ...32-A1	Calabogie ...134-A4	Cedar Point ...45-C2	Clear Lake ...46-C1
Brébeuf ...135-B2	Caledon ...53-B2	Cedarhurst Park ...61-A4	Clearwater Bay ...14-A2
Brechin ...47-A3	Caledon East ...53-B2	Cedarville ...21-B4	Clementson ...14-B4
Breckenridge ...31-A4	Caledonia ...58-A2	Central Patricia ...10-A2	Cléricy ...115-B2
Breckenridge ...134-B3	Caliper Lake ...14-C3	Ceylon ...52-B1	Clermont ...115-A1
Brent ...28-A4	Callander ...27-A4	Chalk River ...29-A4	Clermont ...121-C3
Breslau ...52-C4	Callum ...25-B4	Chalk River ...133-B2	Clerval ...115-A1
Brevort ...21-A4	Calstock ...18-A1	Chambers Corners ...58-C2	Cleveland ...137-C2
Bridgenorth ...47-C3	Calton ...57-A4	Chambly ...136-C3	Clifford ...52-A3
Bridgeville ...114-C3	Caluke ...58-A1	Chambord ...120-B2	Clinton ...56-A1
Bright ...57-A1	Calumet ...32-B2	Champ des Gouffres ...91-B3	Cloridorme ...114-B2
Brighton ...48-C4	Calumet ...135-C3	Champlain ...130-A3	Cloud Bay ...16-B4
Brights Grove ...55-B4	Cambridge ...57-B1	Champlain ...136-C4	Cloutier ...20-B2
Brightside ...40-C2	Camden East ...49-C2	Champneuf ...116-B2	Cloutier ...115-B3
Brimley ...21-A3	Camlachie ...55-B4	Chandler ...114-B4	Clova ...118-A3
Brisay ...83-C4	Campbell's Bay ...30-B4	Chapais ...107-A2	Cloyne ...40-A4
Brisbane ...53-A3	Campbell's Bay ...134-A3	Chapeau ...133-C2	Clute ...19-B1
Bristol ...30-B4	Campbellcroft ...48-A4	Chapleau ...18-C3	Coaticook ...137-C4
Bristol ...40-B1	Campbellford ...48-B3	Chaput Hughes ...20-A2	Cobalt ...20-B3
Bristol ...134-B3	Campbellton ...124-A2	Charing Cross ...61-C3	Cobden ...40-A1
Briston ...42-A2	Campden ...58-B1	CHARLESBOURG ...131-A2	Coboconk ...47-B2
Britt ...35-C3	Canaan ...138-A4	Charleston ...41-B4	Coburn Gore ...138-B3
Brockville ...41-C4	Canborough ...58-B2	Charlo ...124-B2	Cochenour ...8-B4
Brodhagen ...56-B1	Canfield ...58-A2	Charlton ...20-A3	Cochrane ...19-B1
Brome ...137-A4	Cann ...119-A4	Charny ...131-A3	Codes Cor. ...50-A2
Bromont ...137-A3	Cannes-de-Roches ...114-C4	Charteris ...30-B4	Codrington ...48-C3
Bromptonville ...137-C3	Cannifton ...49-A3	Charteris ...134-B3	Coe Hill ...48-B1
Bronte ...53-C4	Cannington ...47-A4	Chartierville ...138-A3	Coin-du-Banc ...114-C4
Brooklin ...54-B1	Cantley ...31-B4	CHÂTEAU GUAY ...136-A3	Colborne ...48-C4
Brouseville ...42-A3	Cantley ...134-C3	Château-Richer ...131-A2	Coldstream ...56-A3
Brown Hill ...46-C4	Canton ...42-B3	Chatham ...61-B2	Coldwater ...46-B3
Brownsburg ...135-C2	Cap- d'Espoir ...114-C4	Chatsworth ...52-A1	Collingwood ...45-C4
Brownsburg- Chatham ...32-C2	Cap- St-Ignace ...131-B1	Chaumont ...50-C2	Collins ...16-A1
Brownsville ...57-A3	Cap-à-i'Aigle ...121-C4	Chazel ...115-B1	Collins Bay ...49-C2
Bruce Mines ...21-C3	Cap-au-Renard ...113-A2	Cheapside ...58-A3	Colombourg ...115-A1
Bruce Sta. ...22-A3	Cap-aux-Os ...114-C3	Cheektowaga ...59-B1	Colton ...42-C3
Brucefield ...56-A1	Cap-Chat ...113-A3	Chelmsford ...24-C4	Columbus ...54-B1
Brudenell ...39-B2	CAP-DE-LA-MADELEINE ...130-A3	Chelsea ...31-B4	Comber ...61-B3
Brunner ...56-C1	Cap-des- Rosiers ...114-C3	Chelsea ...134-C3	Combermere ...39-B2
Brussels ...51-C4	Cape de Rosiers ...91-A4	Chenaux ...40-A1	Commanda ...36-C1
Bryanston ...56-B2	Cape Vincent ...50-B2	Chenaux ...134-A3	Compton ...137-C3
Bryson ...30-B4	Caplan ...124-C1	Chénéville ...32-A2	Conestogo ...52-C4
Bryson ...134-A3	Capreol ...19-C4	Chénéville ...135-B2	Conewango Valley ...59-B4
Buckhorn ...47-C2	Capreol ...25-A3	Cheney ...32-A4	Coniston ...25-A4
Buckingham ...31-B3	Cap-Rouge ...130-C2	Chenier ...30-B2	Conmee ...16-B3
Buckingham ...135-A3	Cap-Seize ...113-B3	Chénier ...134-B2	Conn ...52-B2
Buffalo ...59-B2	Capucins ...112-C3	Chepstow ...51-B2	Connaught ...19-C2
Burford ...57-B2	Caramat ...17-B1	Cherry Creek ...59-A4	Consecon ...49-A4
Burgoyne ...51-B1	Cardinal ...42-A3	Cherry Valley ...49-B4	Constance Bay ...41-B1
Burk's Falls ...37-A3	Cargill ...51-C2	Chesley ...51-C2	Constance Lake(I.R.) ...12-A4
Burketon ...54-B1	Cariboo Falls ...14-A1	Chesterville ...42-A1	Contrecoeur ...136-C2
Burleigh Falls ...48-A2	Carignan ...129-C1	Chibougamau ...107-C2	Conway ...49-C3
Burlington ...53-C4	Carleton ...60-A4	Chichester ...29-C3	Cookshire ...138-A3
Burnaby ...58-C2	Carleton ...60-B4	Chichester ...133-C2	Cookstown ...53-B1
Burnstown ...40-B1	Carleton ...124-C1	CHICOUTIMI ...121-A2	Copetown ...57-C1
Burnstown ...134-A4	Carleton Place ...41-A2	Chippawa ...59-A1	Copper Cliff ...25-A4
Burnt Creek ...84-C3	Carleton Place ...134-B4	Chippawa Hill ...51-B1	Corbeil ...27-A4
Burnt Island ...33-A4	Carlisle ...53-B4	Chisasibi ...86-A1	Corbeil ...125-A4
Burpee ...33-B4	Carlow ...51-B4	Christian Island ...45-C2	Corbett ...55-C2
Burritts Rapids ...41-B2	Carlsbad Springs ...31-C4	Chute-à-Blondeau ...32-C2	Corbetton ...52-C1
Burtch ...57-C2	Carlsruhe ...52-A2	Chute-aux- Outardes ...111-C3	Cordova Mines ...48-B2
Burwash ...35-A1	Carnarvon ...47-A1	Chute-Saint-Philippe ...128-A3	Cormac ...39-C2
Buyck ...15-A4	Carp ...14-B4	Clair ...123-A4	Cornwall ...42-C1
Byng ...58-B2	Carp ...41-B1	Clandboye ...56-A2	Cornwall ...135-B4
Byng Inlet ...35-C3	Carrying Place ...48-C4	Clarence ...31-C3	Corthers ...132-C1

Corunna................55-A4
Coteau-du-Lac........136-A4
Cote-Nord-du Golfe du St. Lorent 92-A2
Cottage Park..........21-A3
Cottam................61-A4
Couchiching (I.R.).....14-C3
Coulson...............46-B3
Courtice..............54-B1
Courtland.............57-B3
Courtright............61-A1
Cowansville..........137-A4
Craighurst............46-A3
Cranberry Lake........42-C4
Crane Lake...........15-A4
Crediton.............56-A2
Creemore.............52-C1
Cressy...............49-C3
Crofton..............49-B3
Croftville...........16-A4
Crookston............49-A2
Crosby...............41-A4
Crosshill............52-B4
Croton...............61-C1
Crow Lake............14-B3
Crow Lake............40-C4
Crown Hill...........46-B4
Crysler..............42-A1
Crystal Beach........59-A2
Crystal Falls........20-B4
Crystal Falls........26-B4
Cultus...............57-B4
Cumberland...........31-C4
Cumberland Beach.....46-B3
Curran...............32-A3
Cusson...............15-A4
Cutler...............33-B2
D'Alembert...........20-B1
D'Alembert...........115-B3
Daaquam.............131-C3
Dacre................40-A2
Dafler...............21-B3
Dain City............58-C2
Dalhousie...........124-B2
Dalhousie Mills......32-C3
Dalkeith.............32-C3
Dalrymple............47-A3
Dalston..............46-B4
Damascus.............52-C3
Danford Lake.........30-B3
Danford Lake........134-B2
Danville............137-B2
Darbyville...........53-B4
Darien Ctr...........59-C1
Dartford.............48-B3
Dashwood.............56-A2
Daveluyville........130-B4
Davidson.............30-A3
Davidson............134-A2
Dawsonville.........124-A2
Day Mills............22-B3
Dayton...............22-A4
Dayton...............59-B4
De Kalo..............42-A4
De Tour Village......21-C4
Deacon...............39-B1
Dealtown.............61-C3
Dean Lake............22-B4
Deanlea Beach........45-C3
Dear Taylor..........60-B4
Dearborn.............60-B3
Déception............74-A1
Deep River...........29-A3
Deep River..........133-B2
Deer Lake.............8-B1
Deerbrook............61-A3
Degelis.............122-C4
Delaware.............56-B3
Déléage............127-C4
Delhi................57-B3

Delisle.............120-B1
Delta................41-B4
Demers- Centre......133-C2
Denbigh..............39-C3
Denbigh.............133-C4
Denfield.............56-B3
Dengy Place..........92-B2
Denholm..............31-A3
Denholm.............134-C2
Departure Lake.......19-A1
Desaulniers..........20-A4
Desaulniers..........26-A3
Desbarats............21-C3
Desbiens............120-B2
Desboro..............51-C1
Deseronto............49-B3
Desjardinsville.....133-C2
Desmaraisville......106-B3
Despinassy..........116-B1
Destor..............115-B2
Detroit..............60-B3
Deux Rivieres........28-A3
Deux-Montagnes......136-A3
Deux-Rivières.......125-C4
Devlin...............14-C4
Dexter...............50-C2
Dexter...............50-C3
Dillon...............36-A4
Dinorwic.............15-A2
Disraëli............138-A2
Dixons Corners.......42-A2
Dobbinton............51-C1
Dokis................36-B1
Dolbeau- Mistassini 109-A4
Dome.................19-B2
Domville.............41-C3
Donegal..............52-A4
Donnacona...........130-B3
Donwood..............48-A3
Dorchester...........56-C3
Dorion...............16-C3
Dorking..............52-B4
Dornoch..............52-A1
Dorset...............38-A4
Dosquet.............131-A3
Douglas..............40-A1
Douglastown..........91-A4
Douglastown.........114-C3
Dover Centre.........61-B2
Dowling..............24-C4
Drapeau.............124-B1
Drayton..............52-B3
Dresden..............61-B1
Driftwood............19-B1
Drumbo...............57-B1
Drummond.............21-C4
DRUMMONDVILLE.......137-B2
Drylake..............90-B2
Duart................62-A1
Dublin...............56-B1
Dubuisson...........116-A3
Duclos...............30-C4
Duclos..............134-B3
Duclos Point.........46-C4
Duhamel..............31-C1
Duhamel.............135-A2
Dunchurch............36-C3
Dundalk..............52-B1
Dundas...............57-C1
Dundee..............135-C4
Dunedin..............52-C1
Dungannon............51-B4
Dunham..............137-A4
Dunkirk..............59-A4
Dunns Valley.........22-A3
Dunnville............58-B2
Dunraven............134-A2
Dunrobin.............41-B1
Dunsford.............47-B3

Duntroon.............45-C4
Dunvegan.............32-B3
Duparquet............20-B1
Duparquet...........115-A2
Dupuy................20-A1
Dupuy...............115-A1
Durham...............52-A2
Dusdswell (Bishopton)138-A2
Dutton...............62-B1
Duttona Beach........62-B1
Dwight...............37-C4
Dyer's Bay...........44-A2
Dymond...............20-B3
E. Otto..............59-C4
Eagle................62-B1
Eagle River..........14-C2
Ear Falls............8-C4
Ear Falls............14-C1
Eardley..............31-A4
Eardley.............134-C3
Earlton..............20-A3
East Aldfield.......134-B2
East Aldfield........30-C3
East Angus..........137-C3
East Aurora..........59-C2
East Broughton......131-B4
East Franklin.......137-A4
East Linton..........44-C4
Eastmain.............86-A3
Eastpointe...........60-C3
Eatonville...........62-A2
Eau Claire...........27-B4
Eau Claire..........125-B4
Eberts...............61-C2
Echo Bay.............21-C3
Eckerman.............21-A3
Edenvale.............46-A4
Edgar................46-B3
Edmundston..........123-A4
Edwards..............41-C1
Edwards..............42-B4
Edys Mills...........61-B1
Eel River Crossing..124-B2
Eganville............39-C1
Eganville...........133-C3
Ehkuapustet.........91-A2
Eldee................20-C4
Eldee................27-A2
Eldee...............125-B3
Eldorado.............48-C1
Elfrida..............58-A1
Elgin Mills..........53-C2
Elginfield...........56-B2
Elizabethville.......47-C4
Elk Lake.............20-A3
Ellicottville........59-C4
Elliot Lake..........33-A2
Elliot Lake..........22-C3
Ellisburg............50-C4
Elmira...............52-B3
Elmstead.............60-C3
Elmvale..............46-A3
Elmwood..............52-A2
Elora................52-C3
Elphin...............40-C3
Elsinore.............51-B1
Embar................90-B2
Embro................56-C2
Embrun...............42-A1
Emerald..............49-C3
Emeril...............90-A1
Emeryville...........61-A3
Emo..................14-C4
Empire Corners.......58-B4
Emsdale..............37-B3
Englehart............20-A3
English River........15-C3
Enterprise...........49-B1
Ericsburgh...........14-C4

Erie Beach...........61-C3
Erieau...............62-A3
Erin.................53-A3
Erin Mills...........53-C3
Erinsville...........49-B1
Escuminac...........124-A1
Esker Siding.........85-A4
Espanola.............34-B2
Esprit-Saint........122-C2
Essex................61-A4
Essipit.............122-A2
Ethel................52-A4
Etobicoke............54-A3
Eton Rugby...........15-A2
Évain................20-B2
Évain...............115-A3
Evans Mills..........50-C2
Evansville...........33-B4
Exeter...............56-A2
Fabre................20-B3
Fabre...............125-A2
Faden................85-A4
Fairground...........57-B4
Falconbridge.........25-B4
Falkland.............57-B2
Fallbrook............40-C3
Fanshawe.............56-B3
Farewell.............52-B3
Farley...............30-C1
Farley..............127-C4
Farm Point..........134-C3
Farnham.............137-A3
Farrellton...........31-A3
Farrellton..........134-C3
Fassett..............32-A2
Fassett.............135-B3
Fassifern............32-C3
Fassifern............32-C4
Fauquier.............19-A1
Fawcettville.........49-B3
Fenella..............48-B4
Fenelon Falls........47-B3
Fennell..............53-B1
Fenwick..............58-C1
Fergus...............52-C3
Ferland..............10-C4
Ferland.............121-A2
Ferme-Neuve.........127-C3
Fermont..............89-C2
Ferndale.............44-B3
Ferndale.............60-B3
Feversham............52-B1
Fibre................21-A4
Field................20-B4
Field................26-A3
Finch................42-B1
Fingal...............56-B4
Finmark..............16-A3
Fisherville..........58-A3
Fitzroy Harbour......40-C1
Five Fingerrs.......123-C3
Flackville...........42-A3
Flesherton...........52-B1
Fletcher.............61-B3
Fleurimont..........137-C3
Flintdale............11-C4
Flinton..............49-A1
Floradale............52-B3
Floral Park..........46-C2
Florence.............61-C1
Flower Station.......40-B2
Foldens..............57-A2
Foleyet..............19-A2
Fontanges............83-B4
Fonthill.............58-C1
Foot's Bay...........46-A1
Fordwich.............52-A3
Forest...............55-B3
Forest Home..........46-B3

Forester	55-A3	
Foresters Falls	30-A4	
Forestville	57-C4	
Forestville	111-B4	
Formosa	51-C2	
Forsythe	117-A3	
Fort Hope	10-C2	
Fort Covington	42-C1	
Fort Coulonge	30-A4	
Fort Coulonge	134-A2	
Fort Erie	59-B1	
Fort Erie	59-B2	
Fort George	86-A1	
Fort Irwin	38-B4	
Fort Kent	123-A4	
Fort Severn	1-A1	
Fort Uilliam	29-B4	
Fort William	133-C2	
Forthton	41-C4	
Fort-Mackenzie	79-A4	
Fournier	32-B4	
Fowlers Corners	47-C3	
Fox's Corners	47-B3	
Foxboro	49-A3	
Foymount	39-C2	
Frankford	48-C3	
Franklin	136-A4	
Franklin	137-A4	
Franktown	41-A2	
Frankville	41-B3	
Franquelin	112-A2	
Franz	18-B3	
Fraserdale	13-B4	
Frater	18-B4	
Fredonia	59-A4	
Freelton	53-B4	
Frelighsburg	137-A4	
French River	35-C2	
Frenchville	123-A4	
Froatburn	42-A2	
Frogmore	57-B4	
Fruitland	58-A1	
Fugèreville	20-B3	
Fugèreville	125-A1	
Fullarton	56-B1	
Fulton	58-B1	
Furnace Falls	47-B1	
Gadshill	56-C1	
Gagnon (Abandoned)	89-B3	
Gagnon-Siding	117-B3	
Galetta	40-C1	
Galiote-la-Fourche	91-B4	
Gallichan	115-A2	
Gallix	102-A4	
Gamebridge	46-C3	
Gananoque	50-B1	
Gananoque Jct.	50-B1	
Garden Hill	48-A4	
Garden Village	26-B4	
Garden River	21-C3	
Gardiner	19-B1	
Garson	25-A4	
Gasline	59-A2	
Gaspé	114-C3	
Gatineau	31-B4	
GATINEAU	134-C3	
Gelert	47-B1	
Georgetown	53-A3	
Georgina	46-C4	
Geraldton	17-A1	
Geraldton East	17-A1	
Gesgapegiag	124-B1	
Gesto	60-C4	
Gheen	15-A4	
Gilchrist Bay	48-A2	
Gilford	53-C1	
Gilmor	39-C4	
Girardville	109-A4	
Glammis	51-B2	

Glen Huron	45-C4	
Glen Alda	48-A1	
Glen Allan	52-B4	
Glen Becker	42-A2	
Glen Meyer	57-B4	
Glen Miller	48-C3	
Glen Nevis	32-C4	
Glen Orchard	46-A1	
Glen Tay	41-A3	
Glen Walter	42-C1	
Glen Walter	135-C4	
Glenarm	47-A3	
Glencairn	53-A1	
Glencoe	56-A4	
Glendale	15-A4	
Glendale	21-C2	
Gloucester	31-C4	
Godbout	112-A2	
Goderich	51-A4	
Godfrey	49-C1	
Gods Lake Narrows	3-A2	
Goetzville	21-B4	
Gogama	19-B3	
Gold Centre	19-B2	
Golden Lake	39-C1	
Golden Valley	36-C2	
Gooderham	47-B1	
Gordon Bay	46-A1	
Gore Bay	33-B3	
Gorrie	51-C3	
Goulais Bay	21-B2	
Goulais River	21-B2	
Goverment Landing	14-C3	
Gowanda	59-B3	
Gowanstown	52-A4	
Gowganda	19-C3	
Gracefield	30-C2	
Gracefield	134-C2	
Grafton	48-B4	
Graham	15-C2	
GRANBY	137-A3	
Grand Bend	55-C2	
Grand Falls	14-C4	
Grand Makasti	91-A3	
Grand Makasti	103-B4	
Grand Marais	16-A4	
Grand-Métis	112-A4	
Grand Portage	16-B4	
Grand Valley	52-C2	
Grande-Cascapédia	124-C1	
Grande Point	61-B2	
Grande-Vallé	114-A2	
Grande-Anse	129-C2	
Grande-Rivière	114-C4	
Grandes-Bergeronnes	122-A2	
Grandes-Piles	130-A3	
Grand-Fonds	121-C3	
Grand-Remous	127-B3	
Gran-Mère	130-A3	
Granton	56-B2	
Grants Corners	42-C1	
Grassie	58-B1	
Grassy Narrows	14-B1	
Gravel Hill	32-B4	
Gravenhurst	46-B2	
Greaney	15-A4	
Great Valley	59-C4	
Greely	41-C1	
Green	10-B4	
Green Valley	32-C4	
Green Lane	135-C3	
Green Valley	135-C4	
Greenbank	47-A4	
Greenbush	41-B3	
Greenfield	32-B4	
Greenock	51-B2	
Greens Corner	57-C3	
Greensville	57-C1	
Grégoir Mill	19-A1	

Grenville	32-C2	
Grenville	135-C3	
Grimsby	58-B1	
Gros Mécatina	92-B2	
Gros Morne	113-C2	
Gros Cap	21-A3	
Grosses-Roches	112-C3	
Guelph	53-A4	
Guénette	128-A3	
Guérin	115-A4	
Guilds	62-A2	
Guildwood	54-B2	
Gull Bay	16-B1	
Guthrie	46-B4	
Guyenne	115-C1	
Hagar	25-C4	
Hagersville	58-A2	
Haileybury	20-B3	
Haldimand	114-C3	
Haley Station	40-A1	
Haliburton	38-B4	
Hall Glen	48-A2	
Hallebourg	12-B4	
Hallville	41-C2	
Hamburg	59-B2	
Hamer Bay	37-A4	
Hamilton	57-C1	
Hammond	31-C4	
Hammond	42-A4	
Hampton	54-C1	
Hannawa Falls	42-C3	
Hanover	52-A2	
Harcourt	38-C4	
Hardwood Lake	39-B3	
Harley	57-B2	
Harlowe	40-A4	
Harmony Beach	21-B2	
Harpurhey	56-A1	
Harrietsville	56-C3	
Harrington	56-C2	
Harrisons Corners	42-B1	
Harriston	52-A3	
Harrow	60-C4	
Harrowsmith	49-C2	
Hartington	49-C1	
Harty	18-C1	
Hastings	48-B3	
Hauterive	111-C3	
Havelock	48-B2	
Havelock	136-B4	
Havre Saint-Pierre	91-A2	
Hawk Junction	18-B3	
Hawkesbury	32-B3	
Hawkesbury	135-B3	
Hawkestone	46-C3	
Hawkins Corners	46-B2	
Haysville	57-A1	
Heathcote	45-B4	
Hébertville	120-C2	
Hébertville Station	120-C2	
Hebron	80-C2	
Heckston	41-C2	
Heidelberg	52-C4	
Hemlo	17-C3	
Hemmingford	136-B4	
Henderson	50-C3	
Henderson Harbor	50-C3	
Hensall	56-A1	
Hepworth	44-C4	
Herdman	136-A4	
Heron Bay	17-B3	
Hérouxville	130-A3	
Hervey-Jonction	130-A2	
Hessel	21-B4	
Heuvelton	42-A3	
Heyden	21-B2	
Hibbard	119-A4	
Hickory Corner	56-A3	

Hickson	57-A2	
Highgate	62-A2	
Highland Grove	39-A4	
Hilliardton	20-B3	
Hillier	49-A4	
Hillsburgh	53-A3	
Hillsport	17-C1	
Hilton	48-C4	
Hilton Beach	21-C4	
Hoards	48-C3	
Hockley	53-A2	
Hogansburg	42-C1	
Holbrook	57-A2	
Holiday Harbour	61-B4	
Holland	59-C2	
Holland Centre	52-A1	
Holland Landing	53-C1	
Holmesville	55-C1	
Holstein	52-B2	
Holtyre	20-A2	
Holyrood	51-B3	
Homer	58-C1	
Homestead	21-B3	
Honeywell Corners	49-A3	
Honeywood	52-C1	
Hope Bay	44-B3	
Hopetown	40-C3	
Hornepayne	18-A1	
Horning's Mills	52-C1	
Houseys Rapids	46-C2	
Hovland	16-A4	
Howdenvale	44-B3	
Hoyle	19-C2	
Huberdeau	32-B1	
Huberdeau	135-B2	
Hudson	15-A1	
Hull	31-B4	
HULL	134-C3	
Humphrey	36-C4	
Hunta	19-B1	
Hunter's Point	125-B2	
Huntingdon	136-A4	
Huntingford	57-A2	
Huntsville	37-B4	
Hurkett	16-C3	
Huron Park	56-A2	
Hymers	16-A4	
Hyndford	40-A1	
Iberville	136-C4	
Ice Lake	33-C3	
Ignace	15-B2	
Ilderton	56-B3	
Indus	14-B4	
Industry Solid Depot	22-C3	
Ingersoll	56-C3	
Ingleside	42-B1	
Inglewood	53-B3	
Ingolf	14-A2	
Inkerman	42-A2	
Inukjuak (Port Harrison)	76-B2	
Inverhuron	51-A2	
Inverness	130-C4	
Inwood	55-C4	
Iona	56-B4	
Iona Stn.	56-B4	
Ipperwash Beach	55-B3	
Irish Lake	52-B1	
Iron Bridge	22-B3	
Irondale	47-B1	
Ironsides	38-C4	
Iroquois	42-A2	
Island Falls	13-B4	
Island Lake	21-B2	
Island View	14-C4	
Ivanhoe	49-A2	
Ivy Lea	50-C1	
Jackson	44-C4	
Jacquet River	124-C2	
Janetville	47-B4	

Jarratt ...46-B3
Jarvis ...58-A3
Jasper ...41-B3
Jeannettes Creek ...61-B3
Jellicoe ...17-A1
Jersey Cove ...114-C3
Jogues ...18-B1
Johnstown ...42-A3
Joliette ...136-B2
Jones ...14-B2
JONQUIÈRE ...120-C2
Jordan ...58-C1
Joyceville ...50-B1
Kabetogama ...15-A4
Kagawong ...33-C3
Kahihikuahitet ...91-A2
Kaiatauhikau ...91-C3
Kakabeka Falls ...16-A3
Kakuhipu Kakustshenani ...92-B1
Kaladar ...49-A1
Kamatshiskueut Uhakamehim ...91-A1
Kamatshiskueut Uhakamehim ...91-B1
Kamouraska ...121-C4
Kanata ...41-B1
KANATA ...134-C4
Kangiqsujuaq ...74-C1
Kangirsuk ...75-B4
Kanupiamisat ...92-B1
Karalash Corner ...21-B2
Kasabonika ...4-C3
Kasabonika ...4-C4
Kasabonika ...5-A3
Kashabowie ...16-A3
Katrine ...37-B3
Kauashetshuak ...92-B1
Kawachikamach ...84-C3
Kazabazua ...30-C2
Kazabazua ...134-B2
Keady ...51-C1
Kearney ...37-B3
Kearns ...20-A2
Kebaowek ...125-B3
Kedgwick ...123-C3
Kedgwick River ...123-C3
Keene ...48-A3
Keewatin ...14-A2
Kee-way-win(I.R.) ...8-C1
Kegaska ...91-C3
Kejick ...14-A2
Keldon ...52-C2
Kellys Corner ...40-A1
Kelvin ...57-B2
Kemble ...44-C3
Kemptville ...41-B2
Kemptville ...41-C2
Kenabeek ...20-A3
Kendal ...54-C1
Kenilworth ...52-B3
Kenmore ...41-C1
Kennisis Lake ...38-B4
Kent Bridge ...61-C2
Kentvale ...21-C4
Kerwood ...55-C4
Keswick ...53-C1
Kettle Point ...55-B3
Key Harbour ...35-B3
Key River ...35-C2
Keyano ...87-C1
Keyser ...55-C3
Kiamika ...128-A4
Kilbride ...53-B4
Killaloe ...39-B1
Killaloe ...133-B3
Killarney ...34-C3
Kilmarnock ...41-B3
Kilough ...51-B3
Kilsyth ...44-C4
Kimberley ...52-B1
Kinburn ...41-B1

Kincardine ...51-A2
King City ...53-C2
Kingfisher Lake ...4-C4
Kingfisher Lake ...10-A1
Kingsbridge ...51-A3
Kingston ...50-A2
Kingsville ...61-A4
Kinloss ...51-B2
Kinmount ...47-B2
Kinross ...21-A3
Kintail ...51-A3
Kintore ...56-C2
Kiosk ...27-B4
Kipawa ...125-B3
Kippen ...56-A1
Kirby ...54-C1
Kirbys Corner ...21-B2
Kirk Cove ...40-A4
Kirkfield ...47-A3
Kitchener ...57-B1
Kitchenuhmaykoosib ...4-B3
Kleinburg ...53-B2
Knop Lake Junction ...84-C3
Knowlton ...137-A4
Kohler ...58-A2
Komoka ...56-A3
Kurtzville ...52-A3
Kuujjuaq (Fort-Chimo) ...79-A2
Kuujjuarapik ...81-B3
L'Anse- au-Loup ...92-C1
L' Île Michon ...91-B3
L' Isle-Verte ...122-A2
L'Alverne ...124-A1
L'Amable ...39-B4
L'Ancienne -Lorette ...130-C2
L'Annonciation ...128-B4
L'Anse a Velleau ...91-A4
L'Anse- au-Griffon ...114-C2
L'Anse- de-Roche ...121-C2
L'Anse Pleureuse ...113-C2
L'Anse-à- Valleau ...114-B2
L'Anse-à-Beaufils ...114-C4
L'Anse-à-Fugère ...114-C2
L'Anse-à-la-Croix ...112-B3
L'Anse-Portage ...92-B2
L'Anse-Saint-Jean ...121-C2
L'Ascension ...120-B1
L'Ascension ...128-B3
L'Ascension-de- Patapédia ...123-C2
L'Assomption ...136-B2
L'Avion de la Rivière a-L'Huile ...91-A3
L'Épiphanie ...136-B2
L'Exelos ...91-A3
L'Île-du- Grand-Calumet ...134-A3
L'Ile-Siscoe ...116-A3
L'Ile- Perrot ...136-A3
L'Ile-Nepawa ...115-A2
L'Islet ...131-C1
L'Islet-sur-Mer ...131-B1
L'Orignal ...32-B3
L'Orignal ...135-B3
La Baie ...121-A2
La Baleine ...121-C4
La Bostonnais ...120-A4
La Conception ...128-C4
La Conception ...135-C1
La Corne ...116-A3
La Doré ...119-C1
La Guadeloupe ...131-A4
La Macaza ...128-B4
La Malbaie- Pointe-au-Pic ...121-C4
La Martre ...113-B2
La Minrve ...128-B4
La Morandière ...116-A2
La Motte ...116-A3
La Passe ...30-A4
La Patrie ...138-A3
La Peche ...30-C4
La Pêche ...134-B3

La Plaine ...136-B2
La Pocatière ...121-C4
La Rédemption ...123-B1
La Reine ...20-A1
La Reine ...115-A1
La Romaine ...92-A3
La Salette ...57-B3
La Salle ...60-B3
La Sarre ...20-B1
La Sarre ...115-A1
La Trinité- des-Monts ...123-A2
La Tuque ...130-A1
La Vallée ...14-C4
Labelle ...128-B4
Label-sur-Quévillon ...116-B1
Labrador City ...89-C2
Lac Allard ...91-B2
Lac Baker ...122-C4
Lac Castagnier ...116-A2
Lac Désert ...128-B4
Lac- des-Îles ...127-C4
Lac Édouard ...120-A4
Lac Grosleau ...32-A2
Lac Grosleau ...135-B2
Lac Humqui ...123-B1
Lac Kénogami ...120-C2
Lac- Mégantic ...138-B2
Lac Nominingue ...128-A4
Lac Rapide ...127-A1
Lac Seul ...15-A1
Lac Simon ...31-C2
Lac-à- Beauce ...130-A1
Lac-à- la-Croix ...120-B2
Lac-au- Saumon ...123-C1
Lac-aux- Sables ...130-A2
Lac-Bouchette ...120-A2
Lac-Cayama ...30-B2
Lac-Cayamant ...134-B2
Laccolle ...136-C4
Lac-des- Commissaires ...120-A3
Lac-des Plages ...32-A1
Lac-des- Plages ...135-B2
Lac-des-Aigles ...122-C2
Lac-des-Ecorces ...128-A3
Lac-des-Loupe ...30-C4
Lac-des-Loups ...134-B3
Lac-du-Cerf ...127-C4
Lac-Etchemin ...131-C3
Lac-Gatineau ...127-C3
LACHINE ...136-A3
Lachute ...32-C2
Lachute ...135-C3
Lackawanna ...59-B2
Lac-Saguay ...128-A4
Lac-Sainte-Marie ...134-C2
Lac-Saint-Joseph ...130-C2
Lac-Saint-Paul ...128-A3
Lac-Simon ...116-B3
Lac-Simon ...135-A2
Lac-Ste- Thérèse ...12-B4
Lac-Supérieur ...128-C4
Lac-Supérieur ...135-C1
Lac-Taint-Mari ...30-C2
Ladysmith ...30-B3
Ladysmith ...134-B2
LaFargeville ...50-C2
Laferté ...115-B2
Lafontaine ...136-A2
Laforce ...125-B1
Laforge ...83-A1
Laggan ...32-C3
Lagoon City ...46-C3
Laird ...21-C3
Lake Dalrymple ...47-A2
Lake Helen(I.R.) ...16-C2
Lake Orian ...60-A1
Lake St.Peter ...38-C3
Lakefield ...48-A3
Lakehurst ...47-C2

Lakelet ...52-A3
Lakeport ...55-A4
Lakesite ...56-C2
Lakeview ...135-C2
Lambeth ...56-B3
Lambton ...138-B2
Lanark ...40-C3
Lancaster ...32-C4
Landrienne ...116-A2
Langelier (La Croche) ...119-C4
Langlade ...117-B3
Langton ...57-B4
Languedoc ...115-C1
Laniel ...20-B3
Laniel ...125-A2
Lansdowne ...50-B1
Lansdowne House ...10-C1
Lappe ...16-B3
Larder Lake ...20-A2
Larouche ...120-C2
LASALLE ...136-B3
Latchford ...20-A3
Latchford Bridge ...39-C2
Laterrière ...120-C2
Latta ...49-A2
Latulipe- et-Gaboury ...125-B1
Launay ...115-C2
Laurentides ...136-A2
Laurier-Station ...130-B3
Laurierville ...130-C4
LAVAL ...136-B3
Lavant ...40-B3
Laverlochère ...20-B3
Laverlochère ...125-A1
Lavigne ...26-A4
Lawrenceville ...42-C2
Le Big ...122-C1
Le Gardeur ...136-B2
Le Gros Violon ...91-A3
Le Squatters ...91-C3
Leamington ...61-B4
Leaskdale ...47-A4
Leeburn ...21-C3
Lefaivre ...32-B3
Leith ...45-A4
Leitrim ...135-A4
Lejeune ...122-C4
Lennoxville ...137-C3
Leon ...59-B4
Léry ...136-B3
Les Boules ...112-A4
Les Buissons ...111-C3
Les Eboulements ...121-B4
Les Escoumins ...122-B2
Les Hauteurs ...123-A1
Les Iles Sainte-marie ...92-A2
Les Islets-Caribou ...112-C2
Les Méchins ...112-C3
Levack ...24-B4
LÉVIS ...131-A2
Lexington ...55-A3
Lexington Heights ...55-A3
Lighthouse Cove ...61-B3
Limoges ...32-A4
Linden Beach ...61-A4
Lindford ...14-C4
Lindsay ...47-B3
Linton ...130-B1
Linwood ...52-B4
Lion's Head ...44-B3
Lions ...56-C3
Lisle ...53-A1
Listowel ...52-A4
Listuguj ...124-A2
Litchfield ...30-A4
Little Britain ...47-B4
Little Current ...34-A3
Little New Albion ...59-C4
Little Valley ...59-C4

Little Rapid....22-A3
Littlefork....14-C4
Lively....24-C4
Livonia....60-A3
Lizotte....120-A3
Lobo....56-B3
Lochiel....32-C3
Lochlin....47-B1
Loman....14-B4
Loman....14-C4
Lombardy....41-B3
London....56-B3
Long Beach....58-C2
Long Beach....47-B3
Long Branch....53-C3
Long Fellow....91-A2
Long Lake(I.R.)....17-B1
Long Point....57-C4
Long Port....57-B4
Long Sault....42-C1
Longbow Lake....14-B2
Longford....46-C3
Longlac....17-B1
Longue Pointe de Mingan....91-A3
Longue-Pointe- de-Mingan....103-B3
LONGUEUIL....136-B3
Lonsdale....49-B2
Loraine....50-C3
Lorette- Ville....131-A2
Loretto....53-A2
Loring....36-B2
Lorne Park....53-C4
Lorneville....47-A3
Lorraine....136-B2
Lorrainville....20-B3
Lorrainville....125-A1
Lots-Renversés....122-C3
Louiseville....129-C4
Louisville....61-C2
Louvicourt....116-B3
Low....31-A3
Low....134-C2
Lowbanks....58-C2
Lowther....18-C1
Lucan....56-B2
Lucasville....55-B4
Lucknow....51-B3
Lude....14-A3
Lunar....21-B1
Lunenburg....42-B1
Lurgan Beach....51-A3
Lyn....41-C4
Lyndhurst....41-B4
Lyster....130-B3
M'Chigeeng....34-A4
Maberly....40-C3
Macamic....20-B1
Macamic....115-B1
Macdiarmid....16-C2
MacDowell....8-C2
Mackey....28-C3
Mackey....133-A2
Maclennan....21-C3
MacTier....46-A1
Madawaska....38-C2
Madawaska....123-A4
Madeleine- Centre....113-C2
Madoc....48-C2
Madrid....42-B3
Madsen....8-B4
Magog....137-B3
Magpie....103-A3
Mahtihk Niapaut....91-A3
Maidstine....60-C4
Maitland....41-C4
Malachi....14-A2
Malartic....116-A3
Malden Centre....60-C4
Maliotenam....102-A4

Mallorytown Landing....41-C4
Manawan....128-C2
Manche- d'Épée....113-C2
Manchester....54-A1
Mandaumin....55-B4
Manilla....47-A4
Manitou....102-C3
Manitouwadge....17-C2
Manitowaning....34-B4
Maniwaki....30-B1
Maniwaki....127-B4
Mann Settlement....123-C2
Manneville....115-C2
Mannheim....57-A1
Mannsville....50-C4
Mansonville....137-B4
Maple....53-C2
Maple Grove....136-A3
Maple Island....36-C2
Maple Leaf....39-A3
Maple Valley....52-C1
Mapleton....56-C4
Mar....44-B3
Marathon....17-B2
Margie....14-C4
Maria....124-C1
Mariatown....42-B2
Marieville....136-C3
Marihill....52-C4
Marine City....61-A1
Marionville....42-A1
Markdale....52-B1
Markham....54-A2
Markstay....25-B4
Marlbank....49-A2
Marmora....48-C2
Marsboro....138-B2
Marsoui....113-B2
Marten Falls (I.R.)....11-B2
Marten River....20-B4
Marten River....26-B2
Martindale....31-A3
Martindale....134-C2
Martintown....32-C4
Marville....53-A3
Marysville....49-B3
Marysville....50-A2
Marysville....55-A4
MASCOUCHE....136-B2
Mashkode....21-B1
Mashteuiatsh....120-A1
Maskinongé....129-C4
Massena....42-B2
Massena....42-C1
Massey....34-A2
Masson....31-C4
Masson- Angers....135-A3
Massueville....137-A2
Matachewan....19-C2
Matagami....105-B3
Matane....112-B4
Matapedia....124-A2
Matawatchan....40-A3
Mathers Corners....48-A3
Matheson....19-C2
Matimekosh....84-C3
Mattawa....20-C4
Mattawa....27-C3
Mattawa....125-B4
Mattice....18-C1
Maxville....32-B4
Maxwell....52-C1
Maynard....41-C3
Maynooth....39-A3
Maynooth....133-A4
Mayo....31-C3
Mayo....135-A3
McArthur Mills....39-B3
McGregor....60-C4

McGregor Bay....34-B2
McKay's corners....61-C2
McKellar....36-B4
McKerrow....34-B1
McWatters....115-B3
Mead....18-B1
Meaford....45-B4
Medina....56-C2
Melbourne....56-A4
Meldrum Bay....33-A4
Melissa....37-B3
Melocheville....136-A3
Melrose....56-B3
Memphis....60-C1
Menihek Siding....84-C3
Menneval....123-C3
Mercier....136-B3
Merlin....61-C3
Merrickville....41-B3
Messines....30-B1
Messines....127-B4
Métabetchouan....120-B2
Metagama....19-B4
Metagama....23-C3
Metcalfe....41-C1
Métis-sur-Mer....112-A4
Micksburg....39-C1
Middle Bay....92-C1
Middlebro....14-A3
Middlemiss....56-A4
Middleport....58-A2
Midland....46-A3
Migisi Sahaigan....14-C2
Miguasha....124-B1
Mihanaika....92-A3
Mildmay....51-C2
Milford Bay....46-B1
Milford Haven....21-C4
Millar Hill....37-C3
Millarton....51-B2
Millbank....52-B4
Millbrook....48-A4
Miller Lake....44-A2
Milna....24-C3
Milton....53-B4
Milverton....52-A4
Mimico....53-C3
Minaki....14-A2
Mindemoya....34-A4
Minden....47-A1
Mine Centre....15-A3
Miners Bay....47-B1
Minesing....46-A4
Minett....46-A1
Mingan....91-A2
Mingan....103-B3
Minnitaki....14-C2
Miquelon....106-A4
MIRABEL....136-A3
Mishkeegogamang....9-C3
Missanabie....18-B3
Missisagi River....22-B4
Mississauga....54-A3
Mistamahkuhua....91-C2
Mistissini....107-C1
Mitchell....56-B1
Mitchell's Bay....61-A2
Mitchipicoten River....18-A3
Moffet....125-B1
Moisie....102-B4
Monck....52-C2
Monet....117-C3
Monetville....35-C1
Monkland....32-B4
Monkton....52-A4
Mono Mills....53-A2
Mont- Laurier....128-A3
Mont- Louis....113-C2
Mont Wright....89-C2

Mont-Apica....120-C2
Mont-Apica....120-C3
Montauban- les-Mines....130-B2
Montbeillard....115-A3
Mont-Burn....115-B3
Mont-Carmel....122-A4
Montcerf....127-B3
Montebello....32-A3
Montebello....135-B3
Monteith....19-C1
Mont-Joli....123-A1
Mont-Lebel....123-A1
Montmagny....131-B2
Montpellier....31-C2
Montpellier....135-A2
MONTRÉAL....136-B3
Montreal River....18-B4
Montreal River....21-A1
Montreal Falls....21-B1
Mont-Saint-Michel....127-B3
Mont-Saint-Pierre....113-C2
Mont-St-Hilaire....136-C3
Mont-Tremblant....128-B4
Mont-Tremblant- Village....128-B4
Mooers....136-B4
Moonbean....19-A1
Moore Falls....47-A1
Moorefield....52-B3
Mooresburg....51-C1
Mooretown....55-A4
Moose Creek....32-B4
Moose Factory....13-B2
Moose River....13-A2
Moosonee....13-B1
Moran....21-A4
Morewood....42-A1
Morganston....48-B4
Morin Heights....135-C2
Morpeth....62-A2
Morrisburg....42-A2
Morses Line....136-C4
Morson....14-B3
Mortimers Point....46-A1
Morton....41-B4
Moscow....49-C1
Mossley....57-A3
Mount Carmel....56-A2
Mount Forest....52-B3
Mount Hope....58-A1
Mount Pleasant....47-C4
Mount Salem....57-A4
Mountain....41-C2
Mountain Grove....40-B4
Mt Brydges....56-A4
Mt. Chesney....50-A1
Mt. Clemens....60-C2
Mt.Albert....53-C1
Muirkirk....62-A1
Muncey....56-B4
Munster....41-B2
Murdochville....113-C3
Murillo....16-B3
Muskoka Falls....46-C1
Muskrat Dam....4-A4
Musquaro....91-C3
Myers Cave....40-A4
Myrtle....54-B1
N. Tonawanda....59-B1
Nachvak....80-B1
Nairn....56-A3
Nairn Centre....34-B1
Nakina....11-B4
Nakmistshetshuant....91-C2
Namur....32-A2
Namur....135-B2
Nanticoke....58-A3
Napanee....49-C2
Napierville....136-C4
Natashquan Le Galets....91-B3

Naughton 35-A1
Navan 31-C4
Nédélec 115-A4
Neebish 21-C3
Neigette 123-A1
Nelles Corners 58-A2
Nellie Lake 19-C1
Nephton 48-A2
Nestleton 47-B4
Nestleton Stn. 47-B4
Nestor Falls 14-C3
Nestorville 22-A3
Nett Lake 15-A4
Neustadt 51-C2
New Duham 57-B2
New Dundee 57-A1
New Hamburg 57-A1
New Baltimore 60-C2
New Credit 57-C2
New Dublin 41-C4
New Glasgow 62-B1
New Haven 60-C1
New Liskeard 20-A3
New Lowell 46-A4
New Richmond 124-C1
New Sarum 56-C4
New Wexford 41-C3
Newbliss 41-B3
Newboro 41-A4
Newburgh 49-B2
Newbury 62-A1
Newcastle 54-C1
Newington 42-B1
Newmarket 53-C1
Newport 137-B4
Newry 52-A4
Newton 52-B4
Niagara Falls 59-A1
Niagara-on-the-Lake 54-C4
Nicabong 29-C3
Nicabong 133-C2
Nicman 102-A3
Nicolet 130-A4
Nile 51-B4
Nipigon 16-C2
Nipissing 36-C1
Nitchequon 88-C2
Nobel 36-B4
Nobleton 53-B2
Noelville 35-C1
Nogies Creek 47-C2
Nolalu 16-A4
Norembega 19-C1
Norland 47-A2
Normandale 57-C3
Normandin 120-A1
Normétal 20-A1
Normétal 115-A1
North Lancaster 32-C4
North Woodslee 61-A3
North Augusta 41-C3
North Bay 27-A4
NORTH BAY 125-A4
North Bruce 51-A1
North Buxton 61-C3
North Cobalt 20-B3
North Gower 41-B2
North Lancaster 135-C4
North Monetville 36-A1
North Troy 137-B4
North York 53-C2
Northbrook 40-A4
NorthSpirit Lake 8-C2
Northville 55-C3
Northwest Bay 14-C3
Norton 137-C4
Norval 53-B3
Norwalk 57-A3
Norway Bay 134-B3

Norwich 57-B2
Norwood 42-B3
Norwood 48-B2
Nosbonsing 27-A4
Notre- Dame- de- Pontmain ..31-A1
Notre-Dame- de-la-Merci ...129-A4
Notre-Dame-de-la-Paix 32-A2
Notre-Dame-de-la-Paix 135-B2
Notre-Dame- de-Lorette 109-A4
Notre-Dame- de-Montauban ..130-B2
Notre-Dame- de-Pontmain ...127-C4
Notre-Dame- Des-Champs 31-C4
Notre-Dame- des-Lourdes ...129-B4
Notre-Dame- des-Monts 121-B4
Notre-Dame- du-Laus 31-A1
Notre-Dame- du-Portage 122-A3
Notre-Dame- du-Rosaire 120-C1
Notre-Dame- du-Rosaire 131-C2
Notre-Dame-de- la-Salett ..135-A2
Notre-Dame-de-la-Salette ...31-B3
Notre-Dame-du-Lac 122-C3
Notre-Dame-du-Laus 31-B1
Notre-Dame-du-Laus 134-C2
Notre-Dame-du-Nord 20-B3
Notre-Dame-du-Nord 125-A1
Nottawa 45-C4
Nouvelle 124-B1
Novar 37-B3
Numogate 41-B3
O'Briens Landing 15-B1
Oak Bay 124-A2
Oak Park 60-A2
Oakdale 61-C1
Oakville 53-C4
Oakwood 47-B4
Oba 18-B2
Obaska 116-B3
Obedjiwan 118-B2
Odessa 49-C2
Ogdensburg 42-A3
Ogidaki 21-C1
Ogoki 11-B2
Ohsweken 57-C2
Oil City 55-B4
Oil Springs 61-B1
Oka 136-A3
Old Factory River 86-A3
Old Fort Bay (Vieux-Fort) ..92-C1
Oldcastle 60-C3
Oliphant 44-B4
Omar 50-C1
Omemee 47-C4
Ompah 40-B3
Onaping 57-C2
Onondaga 57-C2
Onslow Corners 30-C4
Onslow Corners 134-B3
Opasatika 18-C1
Ophir 22-A3
Orangeville 53-A2
Orchard Park 59-C2
Oreway 90-B2
Orland 48-C4
Orléans 31-B4
Ormsby 39-B4
Ormstown 136-A4
Oro Station 46-B4
Orono 54-C1
Orr 15-A4
Orr Lake 46-A3
Orrville 36-C4
Orton 53-A3
Orwell 56-C4
Osceola 39-C1
Osgoode 41-C1
Oshawa 54-C1
Oskélanéo 118-A3

Osnabruck Centre 42-B1
Ossossane Beach 45-C3
Ostrander 57-A3
Ostryhon Corners 58-C2
Other Rapids 13-A3
Ottawa 31-B4
OTTAWA 134-C3
Otter Lake 30-B3
Otter Lake 134-A2
Otterville 57-B3
Ouellette 35-C1
Ouimet 16-C3
Oujé- Bougoumou 107-A2
Outlet 50-B1
Owen Sound 44-C4
Oxdrift 14-C2
Oxenden 44-C4
Oxford Centre 57-A2
Oxford Mills 41-C2
Oxley 60-C4
Ozark 21-A4
Pabos 114-C4
Pabos Mills 114-B4
Packington 122-C4
Padoue 123-A1
Pagwa River 11-C4
Pain Court 61-B2
Paisley 51-B1
Pakenham 40-C1
Pakuashipi 92-B2
Palmarolle 20-A1
Palmarolle 115-A2
Palmer Rapids 39-B2
Palmerston 52-B3
Palmyra 62-A2
Pangis 21-C1
Papinachois 111-B3
Papineauville 32-A3
Papineauville 135-B3
Paquette Corners 60-C4
Paradis 117-A3
Paradise 21-A2
Pare-Johan Beetz 91-B3
Parent 118-B4
Parham 40-C4
Paris 57-C3
Park Head 44-B4
Parker 52-C3
Parkhill 56-A3
Parkinson 22-B3
Parry Island 36-B4
Parry Sound 36-B4
Parteidge Ponds Ground 92-B1
Pass Lake 16-C3
Patauau Tshuap 91-A3
Paudash 39-A4
Payment 21-B3
Peawanuck 5-C1
Pefferlaw 46-C4
Pelland 14-C4
Pembroke 29-C4
Pembroke 59-C1
Pembroke 133-C2
Pendleton 32-A4
Penouille 114-B3
Pentanguishene 45-C3
Perce 91-A4
Percé 114-C4
Perch River 50-C2
Perdrix Garden 92-C1
Péribonka 120-B1
Perrault Falls 14-C1
Perry 18-B3
Perth 41-A3
Perth Road 50-A1
Petawawa 29-B4
Petawawa 133-B2
Petawawa Point 29-B4
Peterbell 18-C2

Peterborough 47-C3
Pethericks Corners 48-C2
Petit- Cap. 114-B2
Petit Pabos 114-B4
Petite- Matane 112-B4
Petite- Vallée 114-A2
Petite-Anse 114-A2
Petite-Rivière- Saint-François 131-B1
Petites- Bergeronnes 122-A2
Petit-Saguenay 121-C2
Petrolia 55-B4
Phelpston 46-A4
Phillipburg 57-A1
Pic Mobert South(I.R.) 17-C3
Pic River 17-B3
Pickering 54-B2
Pickford 21-B4
Pickle Lake 10-A2
Picton 49-B4
Pied-du-Lac 122-C4
Pigeon River 16-A4
Pikangikum 8-B3
Pike Bay 44-B3
Pikogan 116-A2
Pincourt 136-A3
Pine Hill 32-C2
Pine Portage 16-C2
Pine River 51-A3
Pinehurst 61-C2
Pinewood 14-B3
Pinkerton 51-B2
Piopolis 138-B3
Pitaga 90-B2
Pitt 14-B4
Pittston 42-A2
Plainfield 49-A3
Plaisance 135-A3
Plantagenet 32-A3
Plattsville 57-A1
Pleasant Cors. 135-B3
Pleasant Point 47-B3
Plessis 50-C1
Plessisville 130-C4
Plevna 40-A3
Plummer 21-C3
Pohéné Gamook 122-B4
Point 14-A3
Point Edward 55-A4
Point Alexander 29-A3
Point Alexander 133-B2
Point Carleton 91-B3
Point Clark 51-A3
Point Comfort 30-C2
Point Comfort 134-C2
Pointe de Ouest 91-A3
Point St Pierre 114-C3
Pointe au Baril Station 36-A3
Pointe au Baril 36-A4
Pointe au Cormoran 91-C4
Pointe- Calumet 136-A3
Pointe- du-Lac 130-A4
Pointe- Fortune 32-C3
Pointe Parent 91-C3
Pointe Sud 91-B4
Pointe Aux Pins 21-A3
Pointe-à- la-Croix. 124-A2
Pointe-à- la-Garde 124-A1
Pointe-à- la- Frégate. 114-A2
Pointe-au- Chêne 32-B2
Pointe-au- Chêne 135-B3
Pointe-au-Boisvert 122-A1
Pointe-aux- Anglais 112-C1
Pointe-aux-Outardes 111-A3
Pointe-Jaune 114-B2
Pointe-Label 112-A3
Poissant 128-A3
Poland 40-C3
Poltimore 31-A3
Poltimore 134-C2

Pontiac............................31-A4
Pontiac............................60-A2
Pontiac..........................134-C3
Pont-Rouge....................130-C2
Poole...............................52-B4
Pope Mill.........................42-A4
Poplar Hill........................56-A3
Poplar Dale......................21-C3
Porcupine.........................19-B2
Porquis Junction...............19-C1
Port Carling......................46-A1
Port Sandfield..................46-A1
Port Albert........................51-A4
Port Alexandria................50-A2
Port Alma.........................61-C3
Port Bolster......................46-C4
Port Bruce........................57-A4
Port Burwell.....................57-A4
Port Colborne...................58-C2
Port Credit........................53-C3
Port de Menier.................91-A3
Port Dover........................57-C3
Port Elgin.........................51-B1
Port Franks.......................56-C2
Port Glasgow....................62-B1
Port Huron........................55-A4
Port Lambton....................61-A1
Port Loring.......................36-B2
Port Maitland....................58-B2
Port McNicoll....................46-A2
Port Perry.........................54-A1
Port Rowan.......................57-C4
Port Ryerse.......................57-C3
Port Sanilac......................55-A2
Port Sanilac......................55-A3
Port Stanley......................56-C4
Port Sydney.......................37-B4
Portage du Fort................30-A4
Portage-du-Fort..............134-A3
Port-au-Persil.................121-C3
Port-aux-Quilles.............122-A3
Port-Cartier....................101-C4
Portland Chantry,.............41-B4
Port-Menier....................103-B4
Port-Nouveau-Québec.....79-C2
Potsdam...........................42-C3
Pottageville.......................53-B2
Poularies........................115-B2
Poularies...........................20-B1
Powassan.........................37-A1
Prairie Siding...................61-B3
Preissac..........................115-C2
Premio..............................90-B4
Premio.............................102-B1
Prescott............................42-A3
Press...............................117-A3
Price...............................112-A4
Prices Corner...................46-B3
Priceville..........................52-B1
Primrose...........................52-C2
Prince Albert.....................54-B1
Princeton..........................57-A2
Princeville.......................130-C4
Pronto East......................33-A3
Pronto East......................22-C4
Proton Station..................52-B1
Providence Bay................43-A1
Pt. Stanton.......................46-B2
Pte Verte........................124-C2
Pte-au-Père....................122-C1
Puce.................................61-A3
Pulaski..............................50-C4
Purdy................................39-A3
Purtuniq............................74-A1
Qirnirauajuq......................79-A2
Quaqtaq...........................75-B3
QUÉBEC.........................131-A2
Queensborough................48-C1
Quibell..............................14-C1

Quisibis..........................123-B4
Quyon..............................30-C4
Quyon............................134-B3
Raco.................................21-A3
Radisson...........................86-B1
Raglan..............................54-B1
Ragueneau......................111-C3
Rainham Centre................58-B3
Rainy River.......................14-B3
Ramah..............................80-B1
Ramore.............................19-C2
Ramsey.............................19-A4
Ramsey.............................23-A1
Rangeley.........................138-C4
Ranger Lake.....................22-A2
Ranier...............................14-C4
Rankin...............................29-C4
Ranoke.............................13-A3
Rapide- Blanc.................119-C4
Rapide- Blanc-Station......119-C4
Rapide- Deux..................115-C4
Rapide-Danseur..............115-A2
Rapide-des-Cèdres.........116-B1
Rapides- des- Joachims....28-C3
Rapides-des-Joachims.....126-B4
Rapide-Sept....................115-C4
Ravenna............................45-B4
Ravenscliffe......................37-B4
Ravenshoe........................53-C1
Rawdon...........................129-B4
Ray...................................15-A4
Raymond Ufford................46-A1
Red Bay............................44-B4
Red Lake............................8-B4
Red Lake Road.................14-C2
Red Rock..........................16-C3
Red Rock..........................21-A2
Redbridge.........................20-C4
Redbridge.........................27-A3
Redbridge.......................125-A4
Redditt..............................14-B2
Redickville........................52-C1
Reeces Corners...............55-B4
Relais-Gabriel...................89-C4
Renfrew............................40-B1
Renfrew...........................134-A3
Rennie..............................14-A2
Renton..............................57-C3
Repentigny......................136-B2
Restoule............................36-C1
Reymondville.....................42-B2
Riceville............................32-B4
Richan..............................15-A1
Richards Landing..............21-C4
Richelieu.........................136-C3
Richford..........................137-A4
Richmond..........................41-B2
Richmond..........................57-A4
Richmond........................137-B2
Richmond Hill...................53-C2
Richmondville...................55-A3
Richmont..........................60-C1
Richville............................42-B4
Rideau Ferry.....................41-A3
Ridge Point......................91-A2
Ridgetown.........................62-A2
Ridgeway..........................59-A2
Rigaud............................135-C3
RIMOUSKI.......................122-C1
Rimouski-Est...................122-C1
Ripney..............................51-B3
Ripon................................31-C2
Ripon................................31-C3
Ripon..............................135-B2
River Valley.......................20-A4
River Valley.......................26-A3
Riversdale........................51-B3
Riverview..........................52-C2
Riverview Heights.............42-A3

Rivière au Renard............114-C2
Rivière au Renard.............91-A4
Rivière au Saumons..........91-B3
Rivière Bell.......................91-B4
Rivière- Bleue.................122-B4
Rivière- Brochu...............101-C4
Rivière Chicotte................91-B4
Rivière de la Chaloupe......91-B4
Rivière- du-Loup.............122-A3
Rivière la Loutre...............91-A3
Rivière- Matawin.............129-C2
Rivière Morris.................114-B3
Rivière Ouelle.................121-C4
Rivière- Pentecôte..........112-C1
Rivière Ste-Marie.............91-A3
Rivière- St-Jean..............103-B3
Rivière St-Paul.................92-C1
Rivière-á- Claure............113-B2
Rivière-à-la Loutre..........114-C1
Rivière-à-Pierre...............130-A2
Rivière-au- Tonnerre.......103-A3
Rivière-aux- Graines.......102-C3
Rivière-aux-Rats.............129-C1
Rivière-Sainte- Marguerite.121-C2
Rivière-Trois- Pistoles....122-B2
Rivington.........................135-C2
Robertsonville.................131-A4
Roberval.........................120-A2
Roblin...............................49-B2
Rochebaucourt...............116-B2
Rochester..........................60-B2
Rochester Hill...................60-B2
Rochester Hills.................60-B2
Rock Forest....................137-B3
Rock Island.....................137-C4
Rock Lake.........................21-C3
Rockford...........................45-A4
Rockland...........................31-C4
Rockland.........................135-A3
Rocklyn.............................45-A4
Rockport...........................50-C1
Rocksborough..................46-C1
Rocksprings......................41-C3
Rockwood.........................53-A4
Rockwood.........................60-B4
Rocky Bay(I.R.).................16-C2
Rodney.............................62-A1
Roebuck............................41-C3
Rollet................................20-B2
Rollet..............................115-A4
Rolphton............................28-C3
Rolphton.........................133-B2
Romeo..............................60-B1
Romulus............................60-A4
Roosevelt..........................14-A3
Roquemaure....................115-A2
Rosedale...........................21-B3
Rosehall............................49-A4
Rosemont..........................53-A1
Roseville...........................60-C2
Roslin...............................49-A2
Ross Bay Jtn.....................90-A1
Rosseau............................37-A4
Rosslyn Village.................16-B4
Rossport...........................17-A2
Rostock.............................56-C1
Rothsay.............................52-B3
Roulier.............................115-A4
Round Lake Centre...........39-A1
Rouses Point..................136-C4
Routhierville.....................123-C1
Rouyn- Noranda...............20-B2
ROUYN- NORANDA.........115-B3
Roxton Falls....................137-B3

Royal Oak.........................60-A2
Rudyard.............................21-A4
Ruisseau Blanc.................91-A3
Ruisseau-à- Rebours.......113-B2
Ruisseau-Castor.............113-A2
Ruisseau-Vert..................111-C3
Rupert.............................134-C3
Ruscom Station................61-A3
Russell..............................42-A1
Rutherford.........................61-B1
Rutherglen........................27-A4
Ruthven.............................61-A4
Rydal Bank.......................22-A3
S. Monroe.........................60-B4
S. Wales...........................59-C2
S.Magnetawan...................36-A3
Sachigo..............................3-C3
Sackets Harbor.................50-C3
Sacré- Coeur...................122-A2
Saganaga Lake.................15-C4
Sagard............................121-C3
Saint Andre-Avellin...........32-A3
Saint- Antoine.................136-A2
Saint- Colomban.............136-A2
Saint- Donat....................123-A1
Saint Elzéar- de-Témiscouata ...122-B4
SAINT- EUSTACHE..........136-A3
Saint- Fulgence...............121-A1
Saint- Georges................131-C4
Saint- Germain................122-A4
Saint- Hilarion.................121-C4
Saint- Jacques................136-B2
Saint- Leandre................112-B4
Saint Louis- de-France....130-A3
Saint Magloire.................131-C3
Saint Maurice de-l'Échouerie...114-B2
Saint- Nicolas.................130-B3
Saint- Onésime d'Ixworth....132-A1
Saint Sauveur des-Monts....135-C2
Saint Sixt..........................31-C3
Saint- Zotiquè.................135-C4
Saint-Adalbert.................132-A2
Saint-Adelme...................112-C4
Saint-Adolphe d'Howard....135-C2
Saint-Adrien....................137-C2
Saint-Agapit...................130-B3
Saint-Aimé- des-Lacs.....121-C3
Saint-Alexandre-de-Kamouraska ......
....122-A3
Saint-Alexandre-des-Lacs....123-C1
Saint-Alexis-de-Matapédia....123-C2
Saint-Alexis- des-Monts....129-C3
Saint-Alphonse................124-C1
Saint-Alphonse- Rodriguez....129-A4
Saint-Ambroise................120-C1
Saint-André.....................122-A3
Saint-André- d'Argenteuil....135-C3
Saint-André- de-Restigouche ... 124-A2
Saint-André-Avellin..........135-B3
Saint-André-du- Lac-Saint-Jean 120-B2
Saint-Anselme.................131-B3
Saint-Antoine-sur-Richelieu....136-B2
Saint-Apollinaire.............130-B3
Saint-Arsène...................122-B3
Saint-Aubert....................131-C1
Saint-Augustin................120-B1
Saint-Augustin- de-Desmaures.130-C2
Saint-Barnabé-Nord........129-C4
Saint-Basile- de-Tableau....121-B2
Saint-Benoît- Labre.........131-B4
Saint-Bernard-sur-Mer....121-C4
Saint-Boniface- de-Shawinigan.129-C3
Saint-Bruno....................120-C2
Saint-Bruno- de-Guigues....125-A1
Saint-Cajetan..................127-C4
Saint-Camille...................137-C2
Saint-Camille- de-Lellis....131-C3
Saint-Cassien-des-Caps....121-B4
Saint-Célestin..................130-A4

Saint-Césaire....................136-C3
Saint-Charles-de-Bourget.........120-C1
Saint-Charles-de-Drummond....137-B2
Saint-Charles-de- Bellechasse..131-B2
Saint-Charles-Garnier............123-A1
Saint-Chrysostome...............136-B4
Saint-Cléophas.................123-B1
Saint-Clet....................135-C3
Saint-Côme..................129-A4
Saint-Côme Linière.............131-C4
Saint-Cyprien..................122-C3
Saint-Cyprien..................131-C3
Saint-Cyrille- de-Wendover 137-B2
Saint-Cyrille-de-l'Islet..........131-C1
Saint-Damase..................112-B4
Saint-Damase- des-Aulnaies....131-C1
Saint-Damase- des-Aulnaies....122-A4
Saint-Damien..................129-B4
Saint-David- de-Falardeau 120-C1
Saint-Denis....................121-C4
Saint-Dominique...............137-A3
Saint-Dominique- du-Rosaire 116-A1
Saint-Donat....................128-C2
Saint-Donat....................135-C1
Sainte- Agnès..................121-C4
Sainte- Anne-des Plaines 136-B2
Sainte- Catherine- de-Hatley....137-C3
Sainte- Hélène.................122-A4
Sainte- Irène..................123-B1
Sainte Julienne................136-A2
Sainte- Marguerite- Marie........120-A1
Sainte- Monique...............120-B1
Sainte- Rita..................122-C2
Sainte- Sabine.................131-C3
Sainte- Sophie.................136-A2
Sainte Thècle.................130-A2
Sainte- Thérèse-de-Gaspé 114-C4
Sainte- Véronique..............128-B4
Sainte-Adèle..................136-A2
Sainte-Agathe- des-Monts......128-C4
Sainte-Agathe- des-Monts......135-C1
Sainte-Anne- de-Portneuf.......122-B1
Sainte-Anne- de-Sorel.........129-C4
Sainte-Anne-de-Beaupré.......131-A1
Sainte-Anne-du-Lac............127-C3
Sainte-Apolline................131-C2
Sainte- Aurélie.................131-C4
Sainte-Catherine-de-la-Jacques-
Cartier......................130-C2
Sainte-Claire..................131-B3
Sainte-Croix..................130-B3
Saint-Edgar...................124-C1
Saint-Edmond.................116-A3
Saint-Edmond.................119-C1
Saint-Édouard- de-Frampton ...131-B3
Saint-Édouard- de-Lotbinière ...130-B3
Sainte-Edwidge...............137-C4
Sainte-Élisabeth- de-Proulx.....109-B4
Sainte-Émélie- de-l'Énergie.....129-A4
Sainte-Famille d'Aumond 127-C4
Sainte-Félicité.................131-C1
Sainte-Flavie..................112-A4
SAINTE-FOY..................131-A2
Sainte-Francoise 122-B2
Sainte-Germaine- Boulé 115-B2
Sainte-Gertrude Manneville....115-C2
Sainte-Hedwidge 120-A2
Sainte-Jeanne-d'Arc............120-B1
Sainte-Jeanne-d'Arc............123-B1
Sainte-Justine.................131-C3
Saint-Eloi....................122-B2
Sainte-Louise.................131-C1
Sainte-Luce..................122-C1
Sainte-Lucie- de-Beauregard 131-C2
Sainte-Marguerite.............124-A1
Sainte-Marie..................131-A3
Sainte-Marguerite- du-Lac-Masson.
...........................136-A2
Saint-Émile- de-Suffolk..........135-B2

Saint-Emile-de-Suffolk.............32-A2
Sainte-Odile...................122-C1
Sainte-Paule..................112-B4
Sainte-Perpetue...............131-C1
Saint-Éphrem- de-Beauce 131-B4
Sainte-Epiphane...............122-B3
Sainte-Rosalie.................137-A2
Sainte-Rose- du-Nord...........121-B2
Sainte-Sabine- Station...........131-C3
Sainte-Thérèse.................136-B3
Sainte-Thérèse- de-la-Gatineau 127-C4
Sainte-Therese-de-la-Gatmeau....30-B1
Saint-Étienne- des-Gres 129-C3
Saint-Eugène..................131-C1
Saint-Eugène- d'Argentenay 109-A4
Saint-Eugène- de-Guigues 125-A1
Saint-Eugène- de-Ladriere 122-C2
Saint-Eugène-de-Chazel 115-B1
Saint-Fabien- de-Panet 131-C2
Saint-Fabien- sur-Mer...........122-B1
Saint-Félicien..................119-C1
Saint-Félix de-Dalquier.........116-A2
Saint-Félix-d'Otis..............121-A2
Saint-Félix-de-Valois...........129-B4
Saint-Ferdinand...............130-C4
Saint-Ferréol-les-Neiges.........131-A1
Saint-Fidéle-de- Mont-Murray...121-C3
Saint-François- de-Madawaska.122-C4
Saint-Francois Montmagny......131-B2
Saint-Francois- Xavier-de-Viger 122-B3
Saint-François-de-Masham 134-B3
Saint-François-de-Sales 120-A2
Saint-Gabriel..................129-B4
Saint-Gabriel-Lalemant.........122-A4
Saint-Gédéon 120-B2
Saint-Gédéon- de-Beauce 138-B2
Saint-Georges 130-A3
Saint-Georges-de-Malbaie 114-C3
Saint-Gérard de-Berry 115-C1
Saint-Gérard- des-Laurentides ..129-C3
Saint-Germain de-Grantham 137-A2
Saint-Gilles...................130-B3
Saint-Guillaume...............137-A2
Saint-Guillaume-Nord..........128-C3
Saint-Henri...................131-A2
Saint-Henri- de-Taillon..........120-B1
Saint-Herménégilde............138-A4
Saint-Hippolyte...............136-A2
Saint-Honoré 121-A1
SAINT-HYACINTHE...........137-A3
Saint-Ignace- du-Lac 129-A3
Saint-isidore..................114-C4
Saint-Isidore..................136-B4
Saint-Jacques- de-Leeds........131-A4
Saint-Jean- de-la-Lande 122-C4
Saint-Jean- de-Matha 129-B4
Saint-Jean- des-Piles 129-C3
Saint-Jean- Port-Joli...........131-C1
Saint-Jean- sur-le-Lac 127-C3
Saint-Jean-Chrysostome 131-A2
Saint-Jean-de-Matapédia 123-C2
Saint-Jerome 136-A2
Saint-Joseph- de-Kamouraska ..122-A4
Saint-Joseph- de-Beauce 131-B3
Saint-Joseph- de-Lepage 123-A1
Saint-Joseph- de-Mékinac 130-A2
Saint-Joseph- de-Sorel 136-C2
Saint-Joseph-de-la-Rive 121-C4
Saint-Jovite 32-B1
Saint-Jovite..................135-C2
Saint-Jules...................124-C1
Saint-Just- de- Bretenieres 131-C3
Saint-Juste- du-Lac 122-C3
Saint-Lambert.................115-A1
Saint-Lambert-de-Lauzon 131-A3
Saint-Léon...................120-C1
Saint-Léonard d'Aston 130-B4
Saint-Léonard- de-Portneuf.....130-B2
Saint-Léon-de-Standon.........131-C3

Saint-Léon-le-Grand 123-B1
Saint-Louis- (du-Ha!Ha!).........122-B3
Saint-Louis- de-Gonzague.......131-C4
Saint-Louis-de-l'Isle- aux-Coudres ....
...........................121-C4
Saint-Irénée 121-C4
Saint-Luc....................112-B4
Saint-Ludger-de-Milot...........109-B4
Saint-Malo...................138-A3
Saint-Marc- de-Figuery.........116-A2
Saint-Marc- du-Lac-Long.......122-C4
Saint-Marc-de-Latour...........111-B4
Saint-Marce 132-A2
Saint-Marcelin.................123-A1
Saint-Martin 131-C4
Saint-Mathier du-Parc..........129-C3
Saint-Mathieu- d'Harricana 115-C2
Saint-Mathieu- de-Rioux........122-B2
Saint-Maurice- de-Dalquier......116-A2
Saint-Méthode................120-A1
Saint-Michel- des-Saints........129-A3
Saint-Michel-de- Bellechasse ...131-B2
Saint-Nazaire.................120-C1
Saint-Nazaire- de Berry........115-C2
Saint-Nice'phre 137-B2
Saint-Octave- de-l'Avenir.......113-A3
Saint-Octave -de-Métis.........123-A1
Saint-Odilon..................131-C3
Saint-Omer...................124-B1
Saint-Omer...................132-A1
Saint-Ours...................136-C2
Saint-Pacôme.................122-A4
Saint-Pamphile................132-A1
Saint-Pascal..................122-A4
Saint-Patrice..................122-A3
Saint-Paul...................136-B2
Saint-Paul- de-la-Croix.........122-B3
Saint-Paul- de-Montminy.......131-C2
Saint-Philémon................131-B2
Saint-Philippe de Ner...........121-C4
Saint-Pierre...................131-A2
Saint-Pierre de Wakefield 31-A3
Saint-Pierre- de-Wakefield 134-C3
Saint-Pierre-de-Sorel...........136-C2
Saint-Placide-de-Charlevoix 121-B4
Saint-Ple....................137-A3
Saint-Prime..................120-A1
Saint-Prosper.................131-C4
Saint-Quentin.................123-C3
Saint-Raymond...............130-C2
Saint-Rémi- d'Amherst 135-B2
Saint-Roch...................115-B4
Saint-Roch- de-l'Achigan 136-B2
Saint-Roch- de-Mékinac........130-A2
Saint-Roch- des-Aulnaies 131-C1
Saint-Roch-de-Richelieu.........136-C2
Saint-Romuald................131-A2
Saint-Siméon.................121-C3
Saint-Sixte...................135-A3
Saint-Stanislas.................109-A4
Saint-Stanislas- de-Kostka 136-A4
Saint-Tharcisius...............112-C4
Saint-Thomas-Didyme.........119-C1
Saint-Tite....................130-A3
Saint-Ubalde..................130-A3
Saint-Urbain..................121-B4
Saint-Venant- de-Paquette 138-A4
Saint-Vianney.................112-B4
Saint-Yvon 114-B2
Saint-Zacharie................131-C4
Saint-Zénon..................129-B3
Sakami.......................87-A1
SALABERRY- DE-VALLEYFIELD ....
...........................136-A4
Salamanca....................59-C4
Salem.......................52-C3
Salford......................57-A3
Salluit.......................79-C1
Salmon Pt....................49-B4

Saltford.......................51-A4
San-Anicet...................135-C4
Sandfield....................34-A4
Sandford.....................54-A1
Sandhurst....................49-C3
Sandy Beach 114-C3
Sandy Cove..................46-C4
Sandy Lake....................8-B1
Sanikiluaq....................81-A1
Sanmaur.....................119-A4
Sante-Hélène- de-Mancebourg. 115-A1
Sapawe.......................15-C3
Sarnia.......................55-A4
Sarsfield......................31-C4
Sauble Beach 44-B4
Sauble Beach North 44-A4
Sauble Beach South 44-B4
Sauble Falls..................44-B4
Sault Ste. Marie...............21-B3
Sault Ste. Marie...............21-B3
Sault-au-Mouton 122-B1
Savant Lake...................15-C1
Sawbill.......................90-A1
Sawlong Bay..................45-C2
Sawyerville...................138-A3
Sayabec.....................112-B4
Scarborough..................54-A2
Schomberg...................53-B2
Schreiber.....................17-A3
Schutt.......................39-B3
Schwartz.....................30-B3
Schwartz....................134-B2
Scone........................51-C1
Scotia.......................37-B3
Scotland.....................57-B2
Scotstown...................138-A3
Seacliffe......................61-A4
Seaforth......................56-A1
Seagrave.....................47-B4
Seahorse.....................90-B2
Searchmont...................21-C2
Sebright......................46-C2
Sebringville...................56-B1
Secord.......................35-B2
Seeleys Bay...................50-A1
Seguanay....................121-A2
Seine River Village 15-A3
Selby........................49-B2
Sennetere...................116-C2
Sept-Îles....................102-A3
Serpent River..................33-B2
Sesekinika....................20-A2
Shabaqua Corners 16-A3
Shabo.......................90-A1
Shakespeare..................56-C1
Shallow Lake.................44-C4
Shamrock....................40-A2
Shanly.......................42-A2
Shannon....................130-C2
Shannonville..................49-B3
Shanty Bay...................46-B4
Sharbot Lake.................41-A4
Sharon.......................53-C1
Shawanaga...................36-A4
Shawinigan..................130-A3
Shawinigan-Sud..............130-A3
Shawville.....................30-B4
Shawville....................134-B3
Shebandowan.................16-A3
Shedden.....................56-B4
Sheenboro...................29-B3
Sheenboro...................133-C2
Shefferville...................84-C3
Sheguiandah 34-A3
Sheguiandah 34-B3
Shelburne....................52-C2
Sheldrake....................103-A3
SHERBROOKE...............137-B3
Sherkston....................59-A2

Sheshegwaning	33-A4	St. Andrews	42-B1	Stokes Bay	44-A3	Thamesville	61-C1
Shetland	61-C1	St. Anns	58-C1	Stone Mills	50-C2	The Gib	92-C1
Shilington	19-C2	St. Athanase	136-C4	Stonecliffe	28-C3	Thedford	55-C3
Shining Tree	19-C3	St. Augustine	92-B2	Stonecliffe	133-A2	Theresa	50-C1
Shipshaw	120-C2	St. Bernardin	32-B3	Stoney Creek	58-B1	Thessalon	22-A4
Shrewsbury	62-A3	St. Catharines	58-B1	Stoney Point	61-B3	Thetford Mines	131-A4
Siant-Damien- de-Buckland	131-B3	St. Clair	61-A1	Stonyridge	48-A2	Thomasburg	49-A2
Silver Dollar	15-C2	St. Clair Beach	61-A3	Stornoway	138-B2	Thornbury	45-B4
Silver Creek	59-A3	St. Clair Shores	60-C2	Stouffville	54-A1	Thornby	30-B4
Silver Hill	57-B3	St. Columban	56-A1	St-Pascal -Baylon	32-A3	Thornby	134-A2
Silver Islet	16-C3	St. Constant	136-B3	St-Paul-du-Nord	122-A1	Thorndale	56-C2
Silver Water	33-A4	St. Elmo	46-B1	Straffordville	57-A4	Thorne	20-C4
Silverdale	14-C4	St. Eugene	32-C3	Stratford	56-C1	Thorne	27-A2
Simcoe	57-C3	St. George	57-B1	Strathburn	62-A1	Thorne	125-B3
Singhampton	52-C1	St. Isidore	32-B4	Strathroy	56-A3	Thornhill	54-A2
Sioux Lookout	15-A1	St. Joachim	61-A3	Stratton	14-B3	Thornloe	20-B3
Sioux Narrows	14-B2	St. Joseph	55-C1	Stratton	138-C3	Thornton	46-B4
Skead	20-A4	St. Marys	56-C2	Streetsville	53-B3	Thorold	58-C1
Skead	25-B3	St. Raphaels	32-C4	St-René- de-Matane	112-C4	Thorold South	58-C1
Slate Falls	9-B3	St. Thomas	56-B4	Strongs	21-A3	Three Mile Bay	50-B2
Sleeman	14-B3	St. Williams	57-C4	Stroud	46-B4	Thunder Bay	16-B3
Smiths Falls	41-A3	St.Agatha	57-A1	St-Simon	122-B2	Thunder Beach	45-C2
Smithville	58-B1	St.Candiac	136-B3	St-Ulric	112-B4	Thurso	31-C3
Smokey Falls	12-C4	St.Catherine	136-B3	Sturgeon Bay	46-A3	Thurso	135-A3
Smooth Rock Falls	19-B1	St.Charles	25-C4	Sturgeon Falls	26-B4	Tichborne	40-C4
Snake Falls	8-B4	St.Clements	52-B4	Sucker Ck. Landing	36-A1	Tika	90-B4
Snake Falls	8-C4	St.-Clotilde- de-Châteauguay	136-B4	Sucker Creek	34-A3	Tika	102-B2
Snelgrove	53-B3	St.Davids	59-A1	Sudbury	25-A4	Tilbury	61-B3
Snow Road Stn.	40-B3	St.Delson	136-B3	Sullivan	116-A3	Tilden Lake	20-B4
Snug Harbour	36-A4	St.Élie-d'fort	137-B3	Sully	122-B4	Tilden Lake	26-B3
Snyder	59-A1	ST.HUBERT	136-B3	Sultan	19-A4	Tillsonburg	57-A3
Sombra	61-A1	ST.JEAN-SUR RICHELIEU	136-B3	Summer Beaver	10-B1	Timiskaming	125-A1
Sonya	47-B4	St-Lambert	136-B3	Summers Corners	57-A4	Tin Cap	41-C4
Soperton	41-B4	St.-Luc	136-C3	Summerstown	42-C1	Tiverton	51-A2
SOREL-TRACY	136-C2	St.Mather -du-Cap	130-A3	Summerstown	135-C4	Toanche	46-A2
South Woodslee	61-A4	St.-Patrice-de-Sherrington	136-B4	Summerstown Station	42-C1	Tobermory	43-C1
South Bay	9-A4	St.Pauls Stn.	56-B1	Sunbury	50-A1	Toledo	41-B3
South Bay	49-C4	St.Rémi	136-B4	Sunderland	47-A4	Tolsmaville	22-B4
South Baymouth	43-A1	St.Thomas- d'Aquin	136-C2	Sundridge	37-A2	Tomiko	20-B4
South Beach	47-C3	St.Timothée	136-A4	Sunnidale Corners	46-A4	Tomiko	26-C3
South Bolton	137-B4	Stackpool	19-B3	Suomi	16-A4	Tomstown	20-A2
South Cayuga	58-B2	Staffa	56-B1	Sutton	46-C4	TORONTO	54-A3
South Gillies	16-A4	Stalwart	21-B4	Sutton	137-A4	Torrance	46-B1
South Gloucester	41-C1	Stampville	42-A2	Swanton	136-C4	Tory Hill	38-C4
South Gloucester	134-C4	St-Anaclet de-Lessard	123-A1	Swastika	20-A2	Tottenham	53-B2
South Middleton	57-B3	Stanhope	137-C4	Sweaburg	57-A2	Tour Chicotte	91-B3
South Mountain	41-C2	Stanley	16-B4	Swift	14-A3	Tourelle	113-A3
South Porcupine	19-B2	Stanstead	137-C4	Swinton Park	52-B2	Tourville	132-A1
South River	37-A2	St-Antonin	122-A3	Sydenham	50-A1	Townsend	58-A3
Southampton	51-B1	Staples	61-B4	Tadoussac	122-A2	Trent River	48-B2
Southfield	60-A3	St-Augustine	92-B1	Talbotville	56-C4	Trenton	48-C4
Southwold	56-B4	Stayner	45-C4	Tamworth	49-B1	Trenton	60-B4
Sowerby	22-A3	St-Basile-le-Grand	136-C3	Tancredia	134-A3	Tring- Jonction	131-B4
Spanish	33-C2	St-Bruno-de-Montarville	136-C3	Tara	51-C1	Trois-Pistoles	122-B2
Sparta	56-C4	St-Christopher- de-Arthabaska	137-C2	Tarzwell	20-A2	Trois-Rivières-Ouest	130-A4
Spencerville	41-C3	St-Clément	122-B3	Taschereau	20-B1	Trois-Saumons	131-C1
Spotswood	30-A4	Ste.Martine	136-B4	Taschereau	115-C2	Trout Creek	37-A1
Spragge	22-C4	Ste-Angéle-de-Mérici	123-A1	Tashiahahtunekamuk	91-A2	Trout Lake	21-A4
Spragge	33-A2	Ste-Anne- des-Monts	113-A3	Tashota	10-C4	Troy	60-B2
Spring Bay	33-C4	Ste-Blandine	122-C1	Tasiujaq	78-C2	Tunis	19-C1
Spring Brook	48-C2	Ste-Félicité	112-C4	Tatlock	40-C2	Tupperville	61-B1
Springfield	57-A3	Ste-Florence	123-C1	Tatlock	40-C2	Turkey Point	57-C4
Springford	57-A3	Ste-Eleuthére	122-B4	Tavistock	56-C1	Tweed	49-A2
Springmount	44-C4	Sterling Hts.	60-B2	Taylor	60-B4		
Springtown	40-B1	St-Eusébe	122-C4	Tecumseh	60-C3	Udora	47-A4
Springvale	57-C2	Stevensville	59-A2	Tee Lake	125-B3	Uffington	46-C1
Springville	59-C3	St-Fabien	122-B2	Teeswater	51-B3	Uhakahat- Shihip	92-A3
Sprucedale	37-A3	St-François- d'Assise	123-C2	Teeterville	57-B3	Uhatnihip	91-A1
Squatec	122-C3	St-Gabriel-de-Rimouski	123-A1	Tehkummah	34-A4	Ullswater	37-A4
St- Athanase	122-B4	St-Honoré- de-Témiscouata	122-B3	Temagami	20-B4	Umiujaq	81-C1
St Basile	123-A4	St-Hubert	122-B3	Temagami	26-A1	Underwood	51-A1
St Jacobs	52-C4	Still River	35-C3	Témiscaming	20-C4	Uneeda	40-C2
St Jacques	123-A4	Stirling	48-C3	Témiscaming	27-A2	Union	56-C4
St Jean de Cherbourg	112-C4	St-Jean -de-Dieu	122-B2	Témiscaming	125-B3	Uniondale	56-B2
St Léonard	123-B4	ST-JULIE	136-C3	Tenoy Bay	21-C4	Unionville	54-A2
St Majorique	114-B3	St-Médard	122-C2	Terrace Bay	17-B3	Uphill	47-A2
St- Théophile	131-C4	St-Moise	123-B1	Tête a la Baleine	92-A2	Upsala	16-A3
St. Jordan	58-C1	St-Noël	112-B4	Teviotdale	52-B3	Uptergrove	46-C3
St. Albert	32-A4	Stoco	49-A2	Tewesbury	130-C2	Utica	54-B1
				Thamesford	56-C3	Utterson	37-B4

Uxbridge	54-A1	Vernon	135-A4
Val Barrette	128-A4	Verona	49-C1
Val- Bélair	130-C2	Verschoyle	57-A3
Val Caron	25-A4	Victoria Harbour	46-A2
Val Côté	18-C1	VICTORIAVILLE	130-C4
Val- des- Monts	31-B4	Vienna	57-A4
Val- des- Bois	31-B3	Villa Nova	57-C3
Val Gagné	19-C1	Village-des-Aulnaies	131-C1
Val Rita	18-C1	Ville-Marie	20-B3
Val Trerese	24-C3	Ville-Marie	125-A1
Val-Brillant	123-B1	Villemontel	115-C2
Val-Clermont	115-A1	Villiers	48-A3
Valcourt	137-B3	Vineland	58-B1
Val-d' Or	116-B3	Vinemount	58-A1
Val-d'Espoir	114-C4	Vinoy	135-B2
Val-David	136-A2	Vinton	134-A2
Val-des- Lacs	128-C4	Virgil	54-B4
Val-des- Lacs	135-C1	Virginia	46-C4
Val-des-Bois	31-B2	Virginiatown	115-A3
Val-des-Bois	134-C2	W. Seneca	59-B2
Val-des-Monts (Perkins)	134-C3	W.bourne	52-C4
Vale Perkins	137-B4	Wabash	61-C1
Valentia	47-B4	Wabigoon	15-A2
Val-Jalbert	120-A2	Wabos	21-C2
Vallée-Jonction	131-A3	Wabush	90-A2
Val-Limoges	127-C3	Waddington	42-B2
Val-Morin	136-A2	Wahnapitae	25-B4
Val-Saint-Gilles	115-B1	Wahnekewaning Beach	45-C3
Val-Senneville	116-B3	Wahwashkesh	36-B3
Val-Viger	128-A3	Wainfleet	58-C2
Van Bruysse	120-B3	Wakefield	31-A4
Van Buren	123-B4	Wakefield	134-C3
Vanastra	55-C1	Wakeham	114-B3
Vandry	119-B4	Wales Ctr.	59-C2
Vanessa	57-B3	Walford	33-C2
Vanier	31-B4	Walkerton	51-C2
Vankleek Hill	32-B3	Wallaceburg	61-B2
Vankleek Hill	135-B3	Wallacetown	62-B1
Vankoughnet	46-C1	Walpole	61-A2
Varennes	136-B2	Walsh	57-C3
Varna	56-A1	Walsingham	57-B4
Varney	52-A2	Walters Falls	45-A4
Vars	31-C4	Waltham	29-C3
Vasey	46-A3	Waltham	134-A2
Vassan	116-A3	Walton	51-C4
Vaudreuil Dorion	136-A3	Wanup	25-B4
Vaughan	53-C2	Wapekeka (I.R.)	4-C3
Vaureal	91-B3	Wardsville	62-A1
Vendee	32-A1	Warina	32-B4
Vendée	135-B2	Warkworth	48-B3
Venise-en-Québec	136-C4	Warminster	46-B3
Vennachar Junction	39-C3	Warren	25-C4
Vennacher	40-A3	Warren	60-B2
Venosta	30-C3	Warroad	14-A3
Venosta	134-B2	Warsaw	48-A3
Vermilion Bay	14-C2	Wartburg	56-B1
Verner	26-A4	Warwick	55-C3
Vernon	41-C1	Warwick	137-C2

Wasaga Beach	46-A4	Wiarton	44-B4
Washago	46-B2	Wilberforce	38-C4
Waskaganish (Fort Rupert)	86-A4	Wilkesport	61-B1
Waskish	14-B4	Wilkwemikong	34-B3
Waswanipi	106-B3	William Packer's Mesh	92-B2
Waterdown	53-B4	Williams	14-A3
Waterloo	52-C4	Williamsford	52-A1
Waterloo	137-B3	Williamstown	32-C4
Watertown	50-C2	Williiamsburg	42-A2
Watford	55-C4	Willow Beach	46-B1
Watsons Corners	40-C3	Willow Beach	60-C4
Waubamik	36-B4	Willow Grove	58-A2
Waubaushene	46-B3	Wilno	39-B2
Waupoos	49-C3	Wilson	55-A2
Wawa	18-B3	Winchester	42-A1
Weagamow Lake	9-B1	Winchester	135-A4
Webbwood	34-A2	Winchester Springs	42-A1
Webequie	5-B4	Windham Centre	57-C3
Weedon-Centre	138-A2	Windigo	119-B4
Welland	58-C1	Windsor	60-C3
Wellandport	58-B2	Windsor	137-C3
Wellesley	56-C1	Wingham	51-B3
Wellington	49-B4	Winneway	125-C1
Wemindji (Vieux-Comptoir)	86-A2	Winona	58-B1
Wemotaci	119-A3	Winthrop	51-C4
Wemyss	40-C3	Winton	15-B4
Wendake Beach	45-C3	Woburn	138-B3
Wendover	32-A3	Wolf Bay	92-A3
Wendover	135-B3	Woodbridge	53-B2
Werner Lake	14-A1	Woodburn	58-A1
West Montrose	52-C4	Woodford	45-A4
West Guilford	38-A4	Woodland Beach	45-C4
West Lake	49-B4	Woodstock	57-A2
West Lorne	62-B1	Woodview	48-A2
Westmeath	29-C4	Woodville	47-A3
Westport	40-C4	Woodville	50-C3
Westree	19-B4	Wooler	48-C3
Westree	24-A1	Worthington	34-B1
Westwood	48-B3	Wright	30-C2
Whapmagoostui (Poste-de-la-Baleine)..		Wright	134-B2
	81-B3	Wroxeter	51-C3
Wharncliffe	22-A3	Wunnummin Lake	10-A1
Wheatley	61-B4	Wyandotte	60-B4
Wheeler's Pt.	14-A3	Wyebridge	46-A3
Whitby	54-B2	Wyevale	46-A3
White Brook	123-C3	Wymbolwood Beach	45-C3
White Lake	40-C1	Wyoming	55-B4
White River	18-A3	Yamachiche	129-C4
Whitechurch	51-B3	Yamaska	137-A2
Whitedog	14-A1	Yarker	49-C2
Whitefish	34-C1	Yatton	52-B4
Whitefish Bay	14-B2	Ycliff	15-C1
Whitefish Falls	34-A2	York	58-A2
Whitefish Point	21-A2	York Centre	114-B3
Whiteney	133-A3	Youngs Point	48-A2
Whitestone	36-B3	Ypsilanti	60-A4
Whitney	38-C2	Zephyr	47-A4
Whitworth	122-B3	Zurich	55-C1

ITMB Publishing Ltd., 12300 Bridgeport Road, Richmond, BC., CANADA V6V 1J5.
Ph: (604) 273-1400   Fax: (604) 273-1488
E-mail: map@itmb.com   Web: www.itmb.com
© ITMB Publishing. 2016   First Edition
Design / Layout by: Yusuke Ujimiya
Edited by Yusuke Ujimiya, Mark Ramsay, Michael Burns, Tran Dinh Cuong
Lan Joyce, Editor in Chief